College English 1

# Challenger

■ 집필진 명단 ■

**김 유 조** (건국대학교 영어영문학과)
**김 종 갑** (건국대학교 영어영문학과)
**안 희 돈** (건국대학교 영어영문학과)
**이 형 식** (건국대학교 영어영문학과)
**임 인 재** (건국대학교 영어영문학과)
**조 정 순** (건국대학교 영어영문학과)
**한 정 임** (건국대학교 영어영문학과)
**허 현 숙** (건국대학교 영어영문학과)
**황 종 배** (건국대학교 영어영문학과)

College English 1

*Challenger*

1판 1쇄 펴낸날 2006년 8월 25일
1판 2쇄 펴낸날 2008년 3월 25일
편저자 영어교재편찬위원회
펴낸이 오 명
펴낸곳 건국대학교출판부
등록 / 제 4-3 호(1971. 6. 21)
주소 / 143-701, 서울시 광진구 화양동 1번지
전화 / (02) 450-3891 ~ 3
팩스 / (02) 457-7202
홈페이지 / http://press.konkuk.ac.kr
e-mail / press@konkuk.ac.kr
책임편집 이 지 은
본문삽화 공 수 진
표지디자인 김 인 혜
찍은곳 동화인쇄(주)
정가 8,000원



**ISBN 978-89-7107-445-9 13740**

College English 1

# *Challenger*

영어교재편찬위원회 편저

건국대학교출판부

# CONTENTS

Unit 01

# Sports and American Values

**Look at the photos and think about the following questions.**

1. What are the names of the different sports shown in the photos? How much do you know about the sports?

2. What are some other sports that you know about? List as many sports as you can. What sports are you interested in? What sports do you want to play? What players do you like most in each sport?

3. What sports do you think Koreans like? Do you know why?

## Vocabulary Preview

Here are some words and phrases from the reading. Put a check mark by the words you know. If you don' t know the meaning of a word, look it up in the dictionary.

| | |
|---|---|
| ___ 1. spontaneous | ___ 2. organized sports |
| ___ 3. illustrate | ___ 4. inspire |
| ___ 5. equality of opportunity | ___ 6. sociologist |
| ___ 7. laboratory | ___ 8. regardless of |
| ___ 9. compete | ___ 10. without regard to |
| ___ 11. as a whole | ___ 12. in turn |
| ___ 13. ethic | ___ 14. ingrain |
| ___ 15. hustle | ___ 16. persistence |
| ___ 17. slogan | ___ 18. virtue |
| ___ 19. religion | ___ 20. mixture |
| ___ 21. patriotism | ___ 22. observe |
| ___ 23. morally | ___ 24. commit |
| ___ 25. collegiate | ___ 26. occupation |

## Skimming for Main Ideas

Read the text one time quickly for the main ideas and put a check mark by the sentence that you think is mentioned in the reading text.

___ a. Organized sports play a role of strengthening a basic value of a society in the minds of people.

___ b. American organized sports lack equality of opportunity for women players.

___ c. Americans believe that competition in sports will play an important role for the future of American society.

___ d. Professional sports in the United States teach young people traditional American values.

# Read

## Sports and American Values

Most social scientists believe that the sports that are organized by a society generally reflect the basic values of that society and attempt to strengthen them in the minds and emotions of its people. Therefore, organized sports have a more serious social purpose than spontaneous, unorganized play by individuals. This is certainly true in the United States, where the three most popular organized sports are football, basketball, and baseball. Nowhere are the ways and words of democracy better illustrated than in sports.

Organized sports are seen by Americans as an inspiring example of equality of opportunity in action. In sports, people of different races and economic backgrounds get an equal chance to excel. For this reason, notes sociologist Harry Edwards, Americans view organized sports as "a laboratory in which young men, regardless of social class, can learn the advantages and rewards of a competitive system." Although Edwards specifically mentions young men, young women also compete in organized sports without regard to their race or economic background. Women's sports are growing in popularity in the United States, and they now have more funding and support at the college level than in the past. The 1996 Olympics provided evidence of the increased interest in women's organized sports. American women won gold medals for several team sports—softball, basketball, soccer, and gymnastics.

The idea of competition is at the very heart of organized sports in the United States. Many Americans believe that learning how to win in sports helps develop the habits necessary to compete successfully in later life. This training, in turn, strengthens American society as a whole. "It is commonly held," says one sports writer, "that the competitive ethic taught in sports must be learned and ingrained in youth for the future success of American business and military efforts."

The competitive ethic in organized sports contains some elements of hard work—often called "hustle," "persistence," or "never quitting"—and of physical courage—being "tough" or having "guts." Slogans are sometimes used to drive home the competitive virtues for the young participants: "Hustle—you can't survive without it." "A quitter never wins; a winner never quits." "It's easy to be ordinary, but it takes guts to excel."

Amateur athletics, associated with schools and colleges, are valued for teaching young people traditional American values. Professional sports, in addition to their profit and entertainment purposes, are seen as providing an example to inspire the young to take part in organized sports. In the process of serving as an inspiration for traditional basic American values, organized sports have become part of what can be referred to as "the national religion," a mixture of patriotism and national pride on the one hand with religious ideas and symbols on the other. Billy Graham, a famous American Protestant religious leader, once observed: "The Bible says leisure and lying around are morally dangerous... sports keep us busy. There are probably more really committed Christians in sports, both collegiate and professional, than in any other occupation in America."

## Reading for Detail

**Test your understanding of this text by filling gap in each blank or answering the multiple-choice reading comprehension questions without looking back at the text. Choose the best answer from the choices listed.**

1. Sports is what shows the ways and words of ________ best.

ⓐ competition

ⓑ democracy

ⓒ sacrifice

2. The 1996 Olympics evidenced that more and more people are interested in ________ organized sports.

ⓐ black people's

ⓑ young men's

ⓒ women's

3. Americans believe that people should be taught the idea of ________ through organized sports.

ⓐ competition

ⓑ nationalism

ⓒ persistence

4. In 1996 Olympics, American women won gold medals for several ________ sports such as basketball, soccer, and softball.

ⓐ field

ⓑ elite

ⓒ team

5. Organized sports can be characterized by elements of hard work called "________" or "persistence" and of physical courage which is "tough" or "having guts."

ⓐ hustle

ⓑ effort

ⓒ strength

6. The primary purposes of professional sports are profit and ________.

ⓐ patriotism

ⓑ entertainment

ⓒ competitiveness

7. In the United States, "the national religion" consists of ________ and religious ideas.

ⓐ patriotism

ⓑ inspiration

ⓒ professionalism

## Comprehension Questions

**Read the text again and answer the following questions.**

1. What are the three most popular organized sports in the United States?

2. What significance do American people place on organized sports?

3. Why is competition through organized sports important to American youth?

4. What elements does the competitive ethic in organized sports contain?

5. What are the differences between amateur athletics and professional sports in the United States?

6. How can organized sports become part of "the national religion" in the United States?

Student No. : ______________________ Name : ______________________

# Expanding Vocabulary

**1** Each sentence contains an underlined word from the text, followed by three definitions. Put an √ next to the best meaning of the word as it is used in the sentence.

1. Organized sports have a more serious social purpose than <u>spontaneous</u>, unorganized play by individuals.

   ___ ⓐ paid for by a particular organization

   ___ ⓑ with a healthy mental and emotional state

   ___ ⓒ without being planned or thought about

2. <u>Hustle</u>, you can't survive without it.

   ___ ⓐ quick effective movement

   ___ ⓑ a very relaxed state of mind

   ___ ⓒ threatening behavior toward someone

3. The competitive ethic taught in sports must be <u>ingrained</u> in youth for the future success of American business.

   ___ ⓐ firmly instilled

   ___ ⓑ extremely dull

   ___ ⓒ permanently inhabited

4. The competitive ethic in organized sports contains some elements of hard work — often called "<u>persistence</u>," or "never quitting."

   ___ ⓐ loyalty to a person or belief

   ___ ⓑ disagreement between people or groups

   ___ ⓒ continuing to do something in a determined way

5. Professional sports are seen as providing an example to <u>inspire</u> the young to take part in organized sports.

___ ⓐ say what will happen in the future

___ ⓑ stimulate someone into activity

___ ⓒ secretly plan with someone to do something

6. Slogans are sometimes used to drive home the competitive <u>virtues</u> for the young participants.

___ ⓐ a high level of skill

___ ⓑ desirable feature

___ ⓒ a new business or activity

7. There are probably more really <u>committed</u> Christians in sports than in any other occupation in America.

___ ⓐ relating to business or making a profit

___ ⓑ loyal to a belief, organization, or group

___ ⓒ containing all the necessary parts, or information

8. In sports, people of different races and economic backgrounds get an equal chance to <u>excel</u>.

___ ⓐ be better than someone or something

___ ⓑ force someone to live in a foreign country

___ ⓒ force someone to leave a place or organization

9. This training, <u>in turn</u>, strengthens American society as a whole.

___ ⓐ one after the other

___ ⓑ on the contrary

___ ⓒ during the time

10. Americans view organized sports as "a laboratory in which young men, regardless of social class, can learn the advantages and rewards of a competitive system."

___ ⓐ concerning a particular subject

___ ⓑ not important in any way

___ ⓒ without being affected by anything else

## 2 Choose the best word to fill in the blank.

1. The two types are very similar and can only be identified by ________ tests.

ⓐ latent ⓑ laborious
ⓒ complaisant ⓓ laboratory

2. The government's attitude to the issue is ________ indefensible.

ⓐ quickly ⓑ morally
ⓒ promptly ⓓ adversely

3. To ________ the point she has done a comparative analysis.

ⓐ illustrate ⓑ pragmatize
ⓒ aggregate ⓓ frustrate

4. The city we are living in is a ________ of old and new buildings.

ⓐ mixture ⓑ combustion
ⓒ conflation ⓓ fracture

5. The woman ________ that it would probably rain.

ⓐ criticized ⓑ acclaimed
ⓒ observed ⓓ proposed

6. You should state your name, age and ________ on the form.

ⓐ credibility ⓑ probation
ⓒ occupation ⓓ sanction

7. We ________ to attractive countryside surrounding you as scenery.

ⓐ attribute ⓑ object
ⓒ opposed ⓓ refer

8. ________ is defined as a principle of right or good conduct.

ⓐ Morale ⓑ Politics
ⓒ Ethic ⓓ Arithmetic

9. We all know that other goods cannot ________ with this in terms of quality.

ⓐ conflict ⓑ compete
ⓒ consent ⓓ consume

10. Racial ________ still seems light-years away.

ⓐ opportunity ⓑ agreement
ⓒ liberty ⓓ equality

# Listen & Write

**Listen to the recorded part of the text and write a one- or two-sentence summary.**

## 1

Organized sports are seen by Americans as an inspiring example of equality of opportunity in action. In sports, people of different races and economic backgrounds get an equal chance to excel. For this reason, notes sociologist Harry Edwards, Americans view organized sports as "a laboratory in which young men, regardless of social class, can learn the advantages and rewards of a competitive system." Although Edwards specifically mentions young men, young women also compete in organized sports without regard to their race or economic background.

---

## 2

The idea of competition is at the very heart of organized sports in the United States. Many Americans believe that learning how to win in sports helps develop the habits necessary to compete successfully in later life. This training, in turn, strengthens American society as a whole. "It is commonly held," says one sports writer, "that the competitive ethic taught in sports must be learned and ingrained in youth for the future success of American business and military efforts."

---

## 3

Amateur athletics, associated with schools and colleges, are valued for teaching young people traditional American values. Professional sports, in addition to their profit and entertainment purposes, are seen as providing an example to inspire the young to take part in organized sports. In the process of serving as an inspiration for traditional basic American values, organized sports have become part of what can be referred to as "the national religion," a mixture of patriotism and national pride on the one hand with religious ideas and symbols on the other.

---

# Writing Assignment

Choose one of the following topics or titles as your unit writing assignment.

1. The Role of Sports in a Society

2. Why do I like (baseball/basketball/football) best?

3. Is competition necessary in sports?

# Unit 02

# The Language of Color Is Not International

Look at the photos and think about the following questions.

1. What is your favorite color? Is there any special reason why you like that specific color?

2. What do the colors red, black, white, and yellow mean? What does each color symbolize?

3. Which color do you think Korean people like the most? How about Chinese or American people? Think about different races and their favorite colors.

## Vocabulary Preview

**Here are some words and phrases from the reading. Put a check mark by the words you know. If you don' t know the meaning of a word, look it up in the dictionary.**

| | |
|---|---|
| ___ 1. spectrum | ___ 2. article |
| ___ 3. scholar | ___ 4. mourning |
| ___ 5. radicalism | ___ 6. wastes |
| ___ 7. grudge | ___ 8. depressed |
| ___ 9. black humor | ___ 10. symbolize |
| ___ 11. universal | ___ 12. usage |
| ___ 13. disagreement | ___ 14. funeral |
| ___ 15. immediate family | ___ 16. concrete |
| ___ 17. spade | ___ 18. symbolism |
| ___ 19. delicate | ___ 20. ruin |
| ___ 21. dispose | ___ 22. treason |
| ___ 23. tan | ___ 24. wasp |
| ___ 25. range | ___ 26. merge |

## Skimming for Main Ideas

**Read the text one time quickly for the main ideas and put a check mark by the sentence that you think is mentioned in the reading text.**

___ a. How language groups view color

___ b. Color symbolism has cultural variation

___ c. Historical meaning in color symbolism

___ d. Use of color in language

# Read

## The Language of Color Is Not International

*How can the language of color not be the same around the world? After all, we all know that there are only seven colors in the color spectrum. In the following article printed in 1968, a language scholar tells about the language of color.*

"Black is the color of mourning." "Red stands for danger or radicalism." "Green is the symbol for envy." "When you are sad, you're blue." "If you are afraid, you are yellow."

Not at all. At least, not outside the English-speaking world. In China and Korea, white is the color of mourning. White is also worn for mourning in other parts of East Asia. In Hong Kong, mourners at a funeral dress in white. In many European countries, however, black is the color of mourning. In Greece, women traditionally wear black for one year if a member of their family dies. If the husband dies, they will wear black for five years. Many women continue to wear black for the rest of their lives. In Russia, red stands for beauty and life. White is the color of the frozen Siberian wastes and holds the meaning of death. In France, "to be green to someone" means not to bear a grudge. And to be depressed is "to have a black humor." In Italy and Germany, you're yellow with envy, not with fear.

What different colors symbolize to different people is anything but universal. A few do have some wide usage since languages borrow from one another. But in general, what a color symbolizes to one culture will be different in another. For example, the Italian expression for "to be in the red" is "to be in the green." They see the color green as hope, not of envy. And hope remains when all else is lost. "Blue Monday" means going back to work to the office worker in the United States. In Germany, it means a long weekend.

Disagreement on color appears to be the case even for concrete objects. What is "red cabbage" to us is "blue cabbage" to the Germans and "black cabbage" to the Italians. What is a "black eye" to us is a "blue eye" to the Germans. And they call the king of spades not the "black king" but the "green king."

Much color symbolism has a partly historical meaning. For example, "white elephant" comes to us from Siam. The white elephant of Thailand is a rare and delicate animal. And it is very very expensive to support. The kings of Siam made presents of white elephants to those of their subjects whom they wished to ruin financially. One could not, of course, sell or otherwise dispose of a royal gift without encouraging the charge of treason.

Many studies have been done on color and how colors are used in various languages. In many languages, certain color words are lacking. They are often taken care of by using a figure of speech. For example, Spanish and Italian have no word for "tan." Tan-colored objects are usually described as "cinnamon-colored" or "milk-and-coffee." Japanese uses "peach-colored" for pink, "tea-colored" for brown, "mouse-colored" for gray, and "wasp-colored" for yellow.

Where we may see one color, other groups may see many different ones. Italian and French have two words for brown and two for gray. Lithuanian uses different words for "gray" as applied to wool, horses, cows, or human hair.

Some interesting studies have even been done on how language groups view the color spectrum or the range of colors that exist. For example, Malay uses *bolong* for both black and dark blue. They use *merah* for both red and brown. Navajo distinguishes between the black of darkness and the black of coal. They merge gray and brown, as well as blue and green. But the Navajo term for "yellow" covers in part what to us would be green. Zulu merges blue and green into a single term, *luhlaza*. Bongo *kamaheke* does duty for both red and yellow. Some unusual ways that colors are classified are those of the Shona of Rhodesia and the Bassa of Liberia. Compare their classifications with yours on the following chart. Do you still think the language of color is international?

English

| purple | blue | green | yellow | orange | red |
|---|---|---|---|---|---|

Shona

| cipswuka | citena | cicena | cipswuka |
|---|---|---|---|

Bassa

| hui | zīza |
|---|---|

## Reading for Detail

**Test your understanding of this text by filling gap in each blank or answer - ing the multiple-choice reading comprehension questions without looking back at the text. Choose the best answer from the choices listed.**

1. When was this article printed?

___ ⓐ 1968

___ ⓑ 1978

___ ⓒ 1988

2. What does red stand for in English?

___ ⓐ sadness

___ ⓑ envy

___ ⓒ radicalism

3. In France, what does 'green to someone' mean?

___ ⓐ to be depressed

___ ⓑ to be healthy

___ ⓒ to not bear a grudge

4. In Italian, what color represents hope?

___ ⓐ red

___ ⓑ green

___ ⓒ white

5. Why does 'white' hold the meaning of death in Russia?

___ ⓐ Because it is the color of frozen Siberian wastes.

___ ⓑ Because it is the color of the snow angel.

___ ⓒ Because it is the color of mourning.

6. In Greece, how long does a widow wear black?

___ ⓐ for one year

___ ⓑ for five years

___ ⓒ for ten years

7. To whom was a white elephant given in Siam?

___ ⓐ to the members of the royal family

___ ⓑ to someone who committed treason

___ ⓒ to someone whom the king wanted to ruin financially

8. In Japanese, how is gray described?

___ ⓐ as cloud-colored

___ ⓑ as mouse-colored

___ ⓒ as ash-colored

## Comprehension Questions

**Read the text again and answer the following questions.**

1. The meaning of colors is not universal, but why do some colors have wide usage?

2. When a certain color word is lacking, what do people do to describe that color?

3. Different cultures describe 'envy' with different colors. Give some examples.

4. How do language groups view the color spectrum? Give some examples.

5. In Italian, green is the color of hope. How does 'being in the green' in Italian come to mean the situation when everything is lost?

Student No. : ______________________ Name : ______________________

# Expanding Vocabulary

**1** Each sentence contains an underlined word from the text, followed by three definitions or synonyms. Put an √ next to the best meaning of the word as it is used in the sentence.

1. Expect to feel angry, depressed and confused. It's all part of the mourning process.

___ ⓐ early in the daytime

___ ⓑ being sad about someone's death

___ ⓒ being very sad

2. It was a curious mixture of radicalism and conservatism.

___ ⓐ a belief that there should be great or extreme social or political change

___ ⓑ energy or heat that comes from a particular source

___ ⓒ a belief that we should not segregate different races

3. There is no doubt it was an accident and I bear no grudges.

___ ⓐ a food made by boiling oats with water or milk

___ ⓑ a type of fashion for untidy clothes

___ ⓒ a strong feeling of anger or dislike

4. He had no concrete evidence.

___ ⓐ a very hard building material

___ ⓑ something that is definite and specific

___ ⓒ an ugly gray area of a city

5. The theater is $500,000 in the red.

___ ⓐ to spend more money than in the bank account

___ ⓑ to waste money

___ ⓒ to earn a lot of money

6. Engine oil cannot be <u>disposed</u> of down drains.

___ ⓐ throw away

___ ⓑ willing to deal with something

___ ⓒ arranged

7. He was executed for <u>treason</u> after he took part in a plot to blow up the British Parliament building.

___ ⓐ crime of betraying your country

___ ⓑ a group of three

___ ⓒ a good reason

8. 'Get up with the lark' is a <u>figure</u> of speech, meaning 'Get out of bed early'.

___ ⓐ number

___ ⓑ an expression to mean something different from their ordinary meaning

___ ⓒ a well-known person

9. <u>Wasp</u> stings are incredibly painful.

___ ⓐ White Anglo-Saxon Protestant

___ ⓑ a black and yellow flying insect

___ ⓒ a sharp sense of humor

10. A wide <u>range</u> of colors and patterns are available.

___ ⓐ a large area of open land

___ ⓑ an old-fashioned metal cooler

___ ⓒ a number of different things of the same general kind

## 2 Choose the best word to fill in the blank

1. We know that there are only seven colors in the color _______.

ⓐ picture ⓑ spectrum
ⓒ range ⓓ rainbow

2. In English, you say you are _______ when you are afraid.

ⓐ yellow ⓑ green
ⓒ blue ⓓ black

3. In Russia red stands _______ beauty and life.

ⓐ by ⓑ for
ⓒ off ⓓ up

4. In France, 'to be green to someone' means not to _______ a grudge.

ⓐ cause ⓑ take
ⓒ get ⓓ bear

5. In Hong Kong, _______ at a funeral dress in white.

ⓐ clients ⓑ guests
ⓒ mourners ⓓ clerks

6. One could not dispose of a royal gift without encouraging the _______ of treason.

ⓐ crime ⓑ plan
ⓒ people ⓓ charge

7. When certain color words are lacking, they are often taken care of by using a _______ of speech.

ⓐ figure ⓑ mode
ⓒ style ⓓ time

8. The Navajo term for "yellow" _______ in part what to us would be green.

ⓐ merges ⓑ tells
ⓒ covers ⓓ takes

9. A study has been done on how language groups view the color spectrum-or the _______ of colors that exist.

ⓐ line ⓑ number
ⓒ kind ⓓ range

10. "_______ Monday" means going back to work to the office worker in the United States, but in Germany, it means a long weekend.

ⓐ Busy ⓑ Long
ⓒ Blue ⓓ Black

# Listen & Write

**Listen to the recorded text and write a two- or three-sentence summary.**

## 1

What different colors symbolize to different people is anything but universal. A few do have some wide usage since languages borrow from one another. But in general, what a color symbolizes to one culture will be different in another. For example, the Italian expression for "to be in the red" is "to be in the green." They see the color green as hope, not of envy. And hope remains when all else is lost. "Blue Monday" means going back to work to the office worker in the United States. In Germany, it means a long weekend.

## 2

Much color symbolism has a partly historical meaning. For example, "white elephant" comes to us from Siam. The white elephant of Thailand is a rare and delicate animal. And it is very very expensive to support. The kings of Siam made presents of white elephants to those of their subjects whom they wished to ruin financially. One could not, of course, sell or otherwise dispose of a royal gift without encouraging the charge of treason.

## 3

Many studies have been done on color and how colors are used in various languages. In many languages, certain color words are lacking. They are often taken care of by using a figure of speech. For example, Spanish and Italian have no word for "tan." Tan-colored objects are usually described as "cinnamon-colored" or "milk-and-coffee." Japanese uses "peach-colored" for pink, "tea-colored" for brown, "mouse-colored" for gray, and "wasp-colored" for yellow.

# Writing Assignment

Choose one of the following topics as your unit writing assignment.

1. Colors represent different emotions in different cultures. What does "yellow" represent in Korean? Support your idea with examples.

2. Languages borrow from one another, thus some cultures share the same expressions. Are there any expression that you think Korean borrowed from other languages?

3. Can you think of examples of color symbolism derived from historical events?

Unit 03

# Poetry and Advertising

**Look at the photos and think about the following questions.**

1. Have you ever written a poem? How do you think a poet is different from ordinary people?

2. Cite some commercial ads which you think best attract people's attention. What are some characteristics of good ads and bad ads?

3. Do you think poetry and advertising are totally different from each other? What common things do you think exist between them?

## Vocabulary Preview

**Here are some words and phrases from the reading. Put a check mark by the words you know. If you don' t know the meaning of a word, look it up in the dictionary.**

| | | |
|---|---|---|
| ___ 1. mention | ___ 2. concede | ___ 3. lofty |
| ___ 4. verbal | ___ 5. autonomous | ___ 6. commerce |
| ___ 7. connotation | ___ 8. deception | ___ 9. fraud |
| ___ 10. vanity | ___ 11. snobbery | ___ 12. hideous |
| ___ 13. wheedling | ___ 14. multitude | ___ 15. apprehension |
| ___ 16. solemn | ___ 17. momentous | ___ 18. affective |
| ___ 19. ambiguous | ___ 20. primitive | ___ 21. primrose |
| ___ 22. benevolence | ___ 23. transitoriness | ___ 24. aristocratic |
| ___ 25. projection | ___ 26. radiant | ___ 27. identification |
| ___ 28. strenuousness | ___ 29. empathize | ___ 30. fluffy |
| ___ 31. imitation | ___ 32. skulduggery | ___ 33. dimension |
| ___ 34. deficient | ___ 35. panegyric | ___ 36. deodorant |

## Skimming for Main Ideas

**Read the text one time quickly for the main ideas and put a check mark by the sentence that you think is mentioned in the reading text.**

___ a. Poetry is usually read and enjoyed by a special group of people who are highly educated and cultured.

___ b. Poetry makes use of connotative values of words, while advertising uses words for its denotative content.

___ c. A copywriter's role is to make an object symbolic of something beyond itself.

___ d. Poetry and advertising both try to control our conduct by shaping our idealization of ourselves.

# Read

## Poetry and Advertising

### The Poet's Function

One does not often mention poetry and advertising in the same breath. Poetry is universally conceded to be the loftiest of the verbal arts. Advertising, on the other hand, is not even an autonomous art; it is but the handmaiden of commerce. Its name carries connotations, often well deserved, of half-truth, deception, and outright fraud, of appeals to vanity, fear, snobbery, and false pride, of radio and television programs hideous with wheedling voices.

There are many more contrasts. The best poetry seems to be fully appreciated only by the few and beyond the comprehension of the many. The best advertising, however, is thought about, laughed over, and acted upon by multitudes. Poetry is, in the general apprehension, something special, to be studied in schools, to be enjoyed by cultivated people who have time for that sort of thing, to be read on solemn or momentous occasions. Advertising is part of everyday life.

Nevertheless, poetry and advertising have much in common. To begin with, they both make extensive use of rhyme and rhythm ("What's the word? Thunderbird!"). They both use words chosen for their affective and connotative values rather than for their denotative content ("Take a puff... it's springtime! Gray rocks and the fresh green leaves of springtime reflected in a mountain pool.... Where else can you find air so refreshing? And where can you find a smoke as refreshing as Salem's?"). William Empson, the English critic, said in his *Seven Types of Ambiguity* that the best poems are ambiguous; they are richest when they have two or three or more levels of meaning at once. Advertising, too, although on a much more primitive level, deliberately exploits ambiguities and plays on words: a vodka is advertised with the slogan. "Leaves you breathless"; an automobile is described as "Hot, Handsome, a Honey to Handle."

But the most important respect in which poetry and advertising resemble each other is that they both strive to give meaning to the data of everyday experience; they both strive to make the objects of experience symbolic of something beyond themselves. Speaking of the untutored, "wild and rude" Peter Bell in the poem of that name, William Wordsworth said:

*A primrose by the river's brim,*
*A yellow primrose was to him,*
*And it was nothing more.*

A poet, however, cannot let a yellow primrose remain merely a yellow primrose; his function is to invest it with meanings. In the poet's eye the primrose comes to symbolize many things; the joy of early spring, his love of his darling Lucy, the benevolence of God, the transitoriness of life, or other things.

Similarly, an advertising writer cannot permit a cake of soap to remain a cake of soap and "nothing more." Whatever the object for sale is, the copywriter, like the poet, must invest it with significance so that it becomes symbolic of something beyond itself-symbolic of domestic happiness (like Van Camp's pork and beans), of aristocratic elegance (like Chanel No.5), of rugged masculinity (like Marlboros); or of solid, traditional American virtues (like Log Cabin syrup). Whether he writes about toothpaste or tires, convertibles or colas, the task of the copywriter is the poeticizing of consumer goods.

### Art and Life

All literary and dramatic enjoyment involves to some degree the reader's imaginative identification of himself with the roles portrayed in the story or play, and his projection of himself into the situations described. The same principles hold for poetry and advertising, of course, reading poetry, we identify ourselves with the characters the poet creates, or with the poet himself. Advertisers also invite us to identify ourselves with the roles they portray. "Put yourself in this picture!"

says the advertiser, showing radiant groups of young people drinking Seven-Up; families wide-eyed with joy as they try out their new Dodge Dart or sit down to their dinner of fried chicken made with new, improved Mazola; aristocratic gentlemen and sportsmen wearing Hathaway shirts; and the lovely young woman who, having found a toothpaste that cleans her breath while it cleans her teeth, is now a happy bride.

The identification which great poets invite us to make requires of the reader both close attention and imaginative strenuousness; it is not everyone who can empathize with Lucifer in Milton's *Paradise Lost* or with "The Ancient Mariner" of Coleridge. The identifications which advertisers invite us to make are easy and pleasant: most of us would like to be as handsome and well-dressed and joyous and radiant as the people in the advertisements. Looking at the four-color picture of the serene mother standing by her Norge washer with spotless children and piles of fluffy towels, the harassed housewife readily dreams herself into the picture and says, "That's for me!" According to the advertisements, happiness is always within reach.

In spite of this marked contrast in the demands which poetry and advertising make upon their audiences, both have the common function of entering into our imaginations and shaping those idealizations of ourselves that determine, in large measure, our conduct. "Life," said Oscar Wilde, "is an imitation of art." Insofar as both poetry and advertising exact this tribute of imitation, they are both, in a real sense, "creative." Outsiders to the advertising business are often surprised and sometimes amused to learn that the art and copy departments of advertising agencies are known as "creative departments" and their head is known as "creative director." The more you think about it, the more appropriate the term becomes-whether or not you approve of what is created.

Let us call this use of verbal magic (or verbal skulduggery) for the purpose of giving an imaginative, symbolic, or ideal dimension to life and all that is in it, poetry. If we speak separately of what we ordinarily call poetry and advertising, let us speak of the latter as sponsored poetry, and of the former as unsponsored poetry.

Using our terms in this way, we see that our age is by no means deficient in poetry, if we include under that term the poetry of consumer goods. We have more access to poetry (or perhaps we should say that poetry has more access to us) than people have had at any other time in history. It is not possible to listen to most radio stations for five minutes, or to television stations for ten, without running into a panegyric for a beer, a spray deodorant, or a chewing gum. Most American large-circulation magazines are so full of sponsored poetry about breakfast foods, hams, electric appliances, clothing, liquor, and automobiles, and this poetry is so lavishly illustrated by the most expensive processes of color- reproduction and printing in order to attract attention, that reading the articles and stories is like trying to do your algebra homework in Times Square on New Year's Eve.

## Reading for Detail

**Test your understanding of this text by filling gap in each blank or answer - ing the multiple-choice reading comprehension questions without looking back at the text. Choose the best answer from the choices listed.**

1. Choose the one that characterizes poetry rightly.

ⓐ appeal to vanity
ⓑ autonomous
ⓒ pride

2. Choose the one that is NOT common in both advertising and poetry.

ⓐ rhyme
ⓑ denotative content
ⓒ ambiguities

3. What is the job of the poet in relation to "a yellow primrose"?

ⓐ to make it beautiful
ⓑ to name it as a yellow primrose
ⓒ to make it meaningful

4. Which is NOT the source of the reader's literary enjoyment?

ⓐ play
ⓑ identification
ⓒ projection

5. Oscar Wilde said, "Life is an imitation of _______."

ⓐ advertisement
ⓑ idealization
ⓒ art

6. Why is our age not deficient in poetry?

ⓐ Because of the existence of advertising.

ⓑ Because many poetry are published.

ⓒ Because people read a lot of poetry.

## Comprehension Questions

**Read the text again and answer the following questions.**

1. In what ways do poetry and advertising differ from each other?

2. What is the most important aspect in which poetry and advertising resemble each other?

3. Why is the copy department of advertising called the "creative department"?

4. Explain what verbal magic is.

5. Why does the author argue that advertising is sponsored poetry?

Student No. : ______________________ Name : ______________________

# Expanding Vocabulary

**1** Each sentence contains an underlined word from the text, followed by three definitions. Put an √ next to the best meaning of the word as it is used in the sentence.

1. One does not often mention poetry and advertising <u>in the same breath</u>.

 ___ ⓐ almost simultaneously ___ ⓑ in the same spirit
 ___ ⓒ in the same act of breathing

2. Its name denotes outright <u>fraud</u>.

 ___ ⓐ reputation ___ ⓑ deception
 ___ ⓒ manipulation

3. Poetry is to be read on solemn or <u>momentous</u> occasions.

 ___ ⓐ tedious ___ ⓑ minute
 ___ ⓒ important

4. The primrose comes to mean the <u>transitoriness</u> of life.

 ___ ⓐ transcendence ___ ⓑ shortness
 ___ ⓒ meaninglessness

5. Marlboros represent <u>rugged</u> masculinity.

 ___ ⓐ polished ___ ⓑ upright
 ___ ⓒ rough

6. Look at the picture of a <u>serene</u> mother.

 ___ ⓐ transparent ___ ⓑ calm
 ___ ⓒ elegant

7. It is not possible to listen to radio stations without running into a <u>panegyric</u> for a beer.

 ___ ⓐ high praise ___ ⓑ affection
 ___ ⓒ advertisement

## 2 Choose the best word to fill in the blank.

1. Man needs a _________ architectural background to save his sanity in today s world

ⓐ chaotic　ⓑ luxurious
ⓒ expensive　ⓓ serene

2. I choose this unpolished, _________ verse.

ⓐ elegant　ⓑ upright
ⓒ rugged　ⓓ transparent

3. An actress's life is usually _________.

ⓐ transitory　ⓑ transcendent
ⓒ minute　ⓓ simultaneous

4. The search for reality is as _________ as the search for god.

ⓐ serene　ⓑ momentous
ⓒ rugged　ⓓ upright

5. Force and _________ are in war the two cardinal virtues.

ⓐ fraud　ⓑ reputation
ⓒ goodness　ⓓ affection

6. At 34 she is an extremely beautiful woman, _________ endowed by nature with a few flaws in the masterpiece.

ⓐ poorly　ⓑ rashly
ⓒ lavishly　ⓓ miserably

7. Hypocrisy is the essence of _________, but all _________ is about the problem of belonging.

ⓐ honesty　ⓑ deception
ⓒ candor　ⓓ snobbery

8. The best poems are _________; they are richest when they have two or three or more levels of meaning at once.

ⓐ simple　ⓑ unified
ⓒ beautiful　ⓓ ambiguous

# Listen & Write

**Listen to the recorded text and write a two- or three-sentence summary.**

## 1

Nevertheless, poetry and advertising have much in common. To begin with, they both make extensive use of rhyme and rhythm ("What's the word? Thunderbird!"). They both use words chosen for their affective and connotative values rather than for their denotative content ("Take a puff... it's springtime! Gray rocks and the fresh green leaves of springtime reflected in a mountain pool.... Where else can you find air so refreshing? And where can you find a smoke as refreshing as Salem's?"). William Empson, the English critic, said in his *Seven Types of Ambiguity* that the best poems are ambiguous; they are richest when they have two or three or more levels of meaning at once. Advertising, too, although on a much more primitive level, deliberately exploits ambiguities and plays on words: a vodka is advertised with the slogan, "Leaves you breathless;" an automobile is described as "Hot, Handsome, a Honey to Handle."

## 2

All literary and dramatic enjoyment involves to some degree the reader's imaginative identification of himself with the roles portrayed in the story or play, and his projection of himself into the situations described. The same principles hold for poetry and advertising, of course, In reading poetry, we identify ourselves with the characters the poet creates, or with the poet himself, Advertisers also invite us to identify ourselves with the roles they portray. "Put yourself in this picture!" says the advertiser, showing radiant groups of young people drinking Seven-Up; families wide-eyed with joy as they try out their new Dodge Dart or sit down to their dinner of fried chicken made with new, improved Mazola; aristocratic gentlemen and sportsmen wearing Hathaway shirts; and the lovely young woman who, having found a toothpaste that cleans her breath while it cleans her teeth, is now a happy bride.

## 3

In spite of this marked contrast in the demands which poetry and advertising make upon their audiences, both have the common function of entering into our imaginations and shaping those idealizations of ourselves that determine, in large measure, our conduct. "Life," said Oscar Wilde, "is an imitation of art." Insofar as both poetry and advertising exact this tribute of imitation, they are both, in a real sense, "creative." Outsiders to the advertising business are often surprised and sometimes amused to learn that the art and copy departments of advertising agencies are known as "creative departments" and their head is known as the "creative director." The more you think about it, the more appropriate the term becomes-whether or not you approve of what is created.

## Writing Assignment

Choose one of the following topics as your unit writing assignment.

1. The Difference between Poetry and Advertising

2. Why do we need poetry for our everyday life?

3. The Magic of Advertising

Unit 04

# Is Love an Art?

Look at the photos and think about the following questions.

1. Talk about any films or novels which describe beautiful love stories. Why do you think love is beautiful?

2. Which would you like to choose, to be loved or to love? How do you think the two are different?

3. Do you think that to love is a matter of learning? What would you like to do in order to experience real love?

## Vocabulary Preview

Here are some words and phrases from the reading. Put a check mark by the words you know. If you don' t know the meaning of a word, look it up in the dictionary.

___ 1. premise
___ 2. peculiar
___ 3. uphold
___ 4. pursuit
___ 5. margin
___ 6. modest
___ 7. faculty
___ 8. spontaneous
___ 9. intermediary
___ 10. conventional
___ 11. contemporary
___ 12. installment
___ 13. domesticity
___ 14. coyness
___ 15. commodity
___ 16. standpoint
___ 17. asset
___ 18. prevail
___ 19. exhilarating
___ 20. facilitate
___ 21. consummation
___ 22. antagonism
___ 23. infatuation
___ 24. competent
___ 25. craving
___ 26. comprise

## Skimming for Main Ideas

Read the text one time quickly for the main ideas and put a check mark by the sentence that you think is mentioned in the reading text.

___ a. People's definition of being lovable
___ b. Falling vs. being in love
___ c. Conventional view of love
___ d. Prevalent attitude about love

# Read

## Is Love an Art?

Is love an art? If so, then it requires knowledge and effort. Or is love a pleasant sensation, which to experience is a matter of chance, something one "falls into" if one is lucky? This little book is based on the former premise, while undoubtedly the majority of people today believe in the latter.

Not that people think that love is not important. They are starved for it; they watch endless numbers of films about happy and unhappy love stories, they listen to hundreds of trashy songs about love—yet hardly anyone thinks that there is anything that needs to be learned about love.

This peculiar attitude is based on several premises which either singly or combined tend to uphold it. Most people see the problem of love primarily as that of *being loved*, rather than that of *loving*, of one's capacity to love. Hence the problem to them is how to be loved, how to be lovable. In pursuit of this aim they follow several paths. One, which is especially used by men, is to be successful, to be as powerful and rich as the social margin of one's position permits. Another, used especially by women, is to make oneself attractive, by cultivating one's body, dress, etc. Other ways of making oneself attractive, used both by men and women, are to develop pleasant manners, interesting conversation, to be helpful, modest, inoffensive. Many of the ways to make oneself lovable are the same as those used to make oneself successful, "to win friends and influence people." As a matter of fact, what most people in our culture mean by being lovable is essentially a mixture between being popular and having sex appeal.

A second premise behind the attitude that there is nothing to be learned about love is the assumption that the problems of love is the problems of an *object*, not the problem of a *faculty*. People think that to *love* is simple, but that to find the right object to love—or to be loved by—is difficult. This attitude has several reasons rooted in the development of modern society. One reason is the great change which occurred in the twentieth century with respect to the choice of a "love object." In the Victorian age, as in many traditional cultures, love was mostly not a spontaneous personal experience which then might lead to marriage. On the contrary, marriage was contracted by convention—either by the respective families, or by a marriage broker, or without the help of such intermediaries; it was concluded on the basis of social considerations, and love was supposed to develop once the marriage had been concluded. In the last few generations the concept of romantic love has become almost universal in the Western world. In the United States, while considerations of a conventional nature are not entirely absent, to a vast extent people are in search of "romantic love," of the personal experience of love which then should lead to marriage. This new concept of freedom in love must have greatly enhanced the importance of the *object* as against the importance of the *function*.

Closely related to this factor is another feature characteristic of contemporary culture. Our whole culture is based on the appetite for buying, on the idea of a mutually favorable exchange. Modern man's happiness consists in the thrill of looking at the shop windows, and in buying all that he can afford to buy, either for cash or on installments. He (or she) looks at people in a similar way. For the man an attractive girl—and for the woman an attractive man—is the prizes they are after. "Attractive" usually means a nice package of qualities which are popular and sought after on the personality market. What specifically makes a person attractive depends on the fashion of the time, physically as well as mentally. During the twenties, a drinking and smoking girl, tough and sexy, was attractive; today the fashion demands more domesticity and coyness. At the end of the nineteenth and the beginning of the last century, a man had to be aggressive and ambitious—today he has to be social and tolerant—in order to be an attractive "package." At any rate, the sense of falling in love develops usually only with regard to such human commodities as are within reach of one's own possibilities for exchange. I am out for a bargain; the object should be desirable from the standpoint of its social value, and at the same time should want me, considering my overt and hidden assets and potentialities. Two persons thus fall in love when they feel they have found the best object available on the market, considering the limitations of their own exchange values. Often, as in buying real estate, the hidden potentialities which can be developed play a considerable role in the bargain. In a culture in which the marketing orientation prevails, and in which material success is the outstanding value, there is little reason to be surprised that human love relations follow the same pattern of exchange which governs the commodity and the labor market.

The third error leading to the assumption that there is nothing to be learned about love lies in the confusion between the initial experience of "*falling*" in love, and the permanent state of *being* in love, or as we might better say, of "standing" in love. If two people who have been strangers, as all of us are, suddenly let the wall between them break down, and feel close, feel one, this moment of oneness is one of the most exhilarating, most exciting experiences in life. It is all the more wonderful and miraculous for persons who have been shut off, isolated, without love. This miracle of sudden intimacy is often facilitated if it is combined with, or initiated by, sexual attraction and consummation. However, this type of love is by its very nature not lasting. The two persons become well acquainted, their intimacy loses more and more its miraculous character, until their antagonism, their disappointments, their mutual boredom kill whatever is left of the initial excitement. Yet, in the beginning they do not know all this: in fact, they take the intensity of the infatuation, this being "crazy" about each other, for proof of the intensity of their love, while it may only prove the degree of their preceding loneliness.

This attitude—that nothing is easier than to love—has continued to be the prevalent idea about love in spite of the overwhelming evidence to the contrary. There is hardly any activity, any enterprise, which is started with such tremendous hopes and expectations, and yet, which fails so regularly, as love. If this were the case with any other activity, people would be eager to know the reasons for the failure, and to learn how one could do better—or they would give up the activity. Since the latter is impossible in the case of love, there seems to be only one adequate way to overcome the failure of love—to examine the reasons for this failure, and to proceed to study the meaning of love.

The first step to take is to become aware that *love is an art*, just as living is an art; if we want to learn how to love we must proceed in the same way we have to proceed if we want to learn any other art, say music, painting, carpentry, or the art of medicine or engineering.

What are the necessary steps in learning any art?

The process of learning an art can be divided conveniently into two parts: one, the mastery of the theory; the other, the mastery of the practice. If I want to learn the art of medicine, I must first know the facts about the human body, and about various diseases. When I have all this theoretical knowledge, I am by no means competent in the art of medicine. I shall become a master in this art only after a great deal of practice, until eventually the results of my theoretical knowledge and the results of my practice are blended into one—my intuition, the essence of the mastery of any art. But, aside from learning the theory and practice, there is a third factor necessary to becoming a master in any art—the mastery of the art must be a matter of ultimate concern; there must be nothing else in the world more important than the art. This holds true for music, for medicine, for carpentry—and for love. And, maybe, here lies the answer to the question of why people in our culture try so rarely to learn this art, in spite of their obvious failures: in spite of the deep-seated craving for love, almost everything else is considered to be more important than love: success, prestige, money, power—almost all our energy is used for the learning of how to achieve these aims, and almost none to learn the art of loving. Could it be that only those things are considered worthy of being learned with which one can earn money or prestige, and that love, which "only" profits the soul, but is profitless in the modern sense, is a luxury we have no right to spend much energy on?

## Reading for Detail

**Test your understanding of this text by filling gap in each blank or answer - ing the multiple-choice reading comprehension questions without looking back at the text. Choose the best answer from the choices listed.**

1. What do majority of people today believe in about love?

___ ⓐ Love is an art.

___ ⓑ Love requires effort.

___ ⓒ Love does not need to be learned.

2. What is the problem of love to most people?

___ ⓐ problem of loving

___ ⓑ problem of being loved

___ ⓒ problem of one's capacity to love

3. What do people mean by being lovable?

___ ⓐ being popular and having sex appeal

___ ⓑ being active and dependant

___ ⓒ being attractive and offensive

4. How was love viewed in the Victorian age?

___ ⓐ It was a spontaneous personal experience.

___ ⓑ It should lead to marriage.

___ ⓒ It was supposed to develop after the marriage.

5. How has the notion of an attractive man changed over time?

___ ⓐ from being coy to social

___ ⓑ from being domestic to aggressive

___ ⓒ from being ambitious to tolerant

6. When two people are in love, what does feeling infatuation actually mean?

___ ⓐ It proves that their love is intense.

___ ⓑ It proves that they were very lonely.

___ ⓒ It proves that it is a miracle.

7. What are the elements of learning how to love?

___ ⓐ infatuation and miracles

___ ⓑ attraction and competence

___ ⓒ knowledge and practice

8. Why do people so rarely master love?

___ ⓐ Because it is hard to find the object.

___ ⓑ Because love is not their ultimate concern.

___ ⓒ Because they deeply crave love.

## Comprehension Questions

Read the text again and answer the following questions.

1. What do people do in order to make themselves attractive?

2. How was a marriage contracted in traditional culture?

3. What do people seek before marriage these days?

4. What is the characteristic of contemporary culture in relation to falling in love?

5. What are the necessary steps in learning any art?

Student No. : ____________________ Name : ____________________

# Expanding Vocabulary

**1** Each sentence contains an underlined word from the text, followed by three definitions. Put an √ next to the best meaning of the word as it is used in the sentence.

1. Our policy has been to <u>uphold</u> the law.

___ ⓐ to lift something up

___ ⓑ to defend or maintain

___ ⓒ to stop

2. He was drunk and not in control of his <u>faculties</u>.

___ ⓐ the teaching staff of a university

___ ⓑ a group of related departments in some universities

___ ⓒ physical and mental abilities.

3. She wanted him to act as an <u>intermediary</u> in the dispute with Moscow.

___ ⓐ a person who passes messages or proposals between groups

___ ⓑ something very urgent

___ ⓒ people in the medical community

4. The government increased prices on several basic <u>commodities</u>.

___ ⓐ movable piece of furniture

___ ⓑ something found in large numbers

___ ⓒ something that is sold for money

5. Her leadership qualities were the greatest <u>asset</u> of the Conversative Party.

___ ⓐ something that creates tension

___ ⓑ something useful to make things successful

___ ⓒ well organized preparation

6. It was <u>exhilarating</u> to be on the road again and his spirits rose.

___ ⓐ very tiring

___ ⓑ very funny

___ ⓒ very exciting

7. The new airport will <u>facilitate</u> the development of tourism.

___ ⓐ to make something easier or more likely to happen

___ ⓑ to indicate a lack of careful thinking

___ ⓒ to enhance criticism

8. There is still much <u>antagonism</u> between trades unions and the oil company.

___ ⓐ hatred or dislike

___ ⓑ instant attraction

___ ⓑ cooperation

9. We've always regarded him as a man of high professional <u>competence</u>.

___ ⓐ an ability to make people happy

___ ⓑ an ability to do something well or effectively

___ ⓒ an ability to make the best decision

10. You may be <u>craving</u> for some fresh air.

___ ⓐ to dig a deep hole underground

___ ⓑ to cry out loud

___ ⓒ to want to have something very much

## 2 Choose the best word to fill in the blank.

1. This book is based on the former premise, while undoubtedly the majority of people today believe in the _______.

ⓐ later ⓑ latter
ⓒ late ⓓ latest

2. Many of the ways to make oneself lovable are the same as _______ used to make oneself successful.

ⓐ that ⓑ they
ⓒ those ⓓ them

3. In _______ of this aim they follow several paths.

ⓐ pursuit ⓑ pursuance
ⓒ pursue ⓓ pursuant

4. This attitude has several reasons _______ in the development of modern society.

ⓐ come ⓑ rooted
ⓒ taken ⓓ why

5. Marriage was concluded on the _______ of social considerations.

ⓐ terms ⓑ basis
ⓒ top ⓓ bottom

6. Our whole culture is based on the appetite for buying, on the idea of a mutually _______ exchange.

ⓐ favors ⓑ favorite
ⓒ favorable ⓓ favoritism

7. "Attractive" means a nice package of qualities which are popular and ________ on the personality market.

ⓐ seeking ⓑ sought after
ⓒ seemed ⓓ seeming

8. The hidden potentialities which can be developed play a considerable ________ in the bargain.

ⓐ amount ⓑ possibility
ⓒ role ⓓ rule

9. This attitude—that nothing is easier than to love—has continued to be the ________ idea about love in spite of the overwhelming evidence to the contrary.

ⓐ prevalent ⓑ prevail
ⓒ prevalence ⓓ prevalency

10. Although I have all this theoretical knowledge, I am by ________ means competent. I shall become a master in this art only after a great deal of practice.

ⓐ all ⓑ no
ⓒ far ⓓ some

# Listen & Write

**Listen to the recorded text and write a two- or three-sentence summary.**

## 1

A second premise behind the attitude that there is nothing to be learned about love is the assumption that the problems of love is the problems of an *object*, not the problem of a *faculty*. People think that to *love* is simple, but that to find the right object to love—or to be loved by—is difficult. This attitude has several reasons rooted in the development of modern society. One reason is the great change which occurred in the twentieth century with respect to the choice of a "love object." In the Victorian age, as in many traditional cultures, love was mostly not a spontaneous personal experience which then might lead to marriage. On the contrary, marriage was contracted by convention—either by the respective families, or by a marriage broker, or without the help of such intermediaries; it was concluded on the basis of social considerations, and love was supposed to develop once the marriage had been concluded.

## 2

The third error leading to the assumption that there is nothing to be learned about love lies in the confusion between the initial experience of "*falling*" in love, and the permanent state of *being* in love, or as we might better say, of "standing" in love. If two people who have been strangers, as all of us are, suddenly let the wall between them break down, and feel close, feel one, this moment of oneness is one of the most exhilarating, most exciting experiences in life. It is all the more wonderful and miraculous for persons who have been shut off, isolated, without love. This miracle of sudden intimacy is often facilitated if it is combined with, or initiated by, sexual attraction and consummation. However, this type of love is by its very nature not lasting.

## 3

This attitude—that nothing is easier than to love—has continued to be the prevalent idea about love in spite of the overwhelming evidence to the contrary. There is hardly any activity, any enterprise, which is started with such tremendous hopes and expectations, and yet, which fails so regularly, as love. If this were the case with any other activity, people would be eager to know the reasons for the failure, and to learn how one could do better—or they would give up the activity. Since the latter is impossible in the case of love, there seems to be only one adequate way to overcome the failure of love-to examine the reasons for this failure, and to proceed to study the meaning of love.

# Writing Assignment

Choose one of the following topics as your unit writing assignment.

1. What is your definition of a lovable person?

2. How do people get married in your culture?

3. What needs to be done to stay in love?

# Unit 05

# Beauty

Look at the photos and think about the following questions.

1. Name some beautiful people around you. Why do you think they are beautiful? What characteristics do they have?

2. What is your idea of "beauty"? Do you try to look beautiful to other people? What are some advantages and disadvantages of being beautiful?

3. Which do you think is more important, inside beauty or outside beauty? Cite some people who are beautiful on the inside.

## Vocabulary Preview

**Here are some words and phrases from the reading. Put a check mark by the words you know. If you don' t know the meaning of a word, look it up in the dictionary.**

| | | |
|---|---|---|
| ___ 1. paradox | ___ 2. seductive | ___ 3. pedagogical |
| ___ 4. splendid | ___ 5. disciple | ___ 6. wary |
| ___ 7. enchantment | ___ 8. facility | ___ 9. deprive |
| ___ 10. adrift | ___ 11. alienate | ___ 12. arbitrary |
| ___ 13. prestige | ___ 14. superficial | ___ 15. masculine |
| ___ 16. equivalent | ___ 17. accumulate | ___ 18. demeaning |
| ___ 19. vestige | ___ 20. pagan | ___ 21. detriment |
| ___ 22. competent | ___ 23. throe | ___ 24. feminine |
| ___ 25. reinforce | ___ 26. immaturity | ___ 27. blemish |
| ___ 28. depreciation | ___ 29. lamentable | ___ 30. conceive |
| ___ 31. renounce | ___ 32. censure | ___ 33. preen |
| ___ 34. clamber | ___ 35. capacity | ___ 36. disparage |
| ___ 37. crude | ___ 38. abridge | ___ 39. prop up |
| ___ 40. mythology | | |

## Skimming for Main Ideas

**Read the text one time quickly for the main ideas and put a check mark by the sentence that you think is mentioned in the reading text.**

___ a. Since the period of Socrates, the concept of beauty has lost its classical ideals of human excellence.

___ b. Beauty is regarded as being essential to women's character and concerns.

___ c. With a small imperfection, men are usually thought to be more good-looking.

___ d. Beauty is just a pleasure, it can never be any type of power.

# Read

## Beauty

For the Greeks, beauty was a virtue: a kind of excellence. Persons then were assumed to be what we now have to call—lamely, enviously—*whole* persons. If it did occur to the Greeks to distinguish between a person's "inside" and "outside," they still expected that inner beauty would be matched by beauty of the other kind. The well-born young Athenians who gathered around Socrates found it quite paradoxical that their hero was so intelligent, so brave, so honorable, so seductive—and so ugly. One of Socrates' main pedagogical acts was to be ugly—and teach those innocent, no doubt splendid-looking disciples of his how full of paradoxes life really was.

They may have resisted Socrates' lesson. We do not. Several thousand years later, we are more wary of the enchantments of beauty. We not only split off—with the greatest facility—the "inside" (character, intellect) from the "outside" (looks); but we are actually surprised when someone who is beautiful is also intelligent, talented, good.

It was principally the influence of Christianity that deprived beauty of the central place it had in classical ideals of human excellence. By limiting excellence (*virtus* in Latin) to *moral* virtue only, Christianity set beauty adrift—as an alienated, arbitrary, superficial enchantment. And beauty has continued to lose prestige. For close to two centuries it has become a convention to attribute beauty to only one of the two sexes: the sex which, however fair, is always second. Associating beauty with women has put beauty even further on the defensive, morally.

A beautiful woman, we say in English, but a handsome man. "Handsome" is the masculine equivalent of—and refusal of—a compliment which has accumulated certain demeaning overtones, by being reserved for women only. That one can call a man "beautiful" in French and in Italian suggests that Catholic countries—unlike those countries shaped by the Protestant version of Christianity—still retain some vestiges of the pagan admiration for beauty. But the difference, if one exists, is of degree only. In every modern country that is Christian or post-Christian, women are the beautiful sex—to the detriment of the notion of beauty as well as of women.

To be called beautiful is thought to name something essential to women's character and concerns. (In contrast to men—whose essence is to be strong, or effective, or competent.) It does not take someone in the throes of advanced feminist awareness to perceive that the way women are taught to be involved with beauty encourages narcissism, reinforces dependence and immaturity. Everyone (women and men) knows that. For it is "everyone," a whole society, that has identified being feminine with caring about how one looks. (In contrast to being masculine—which is identified with caring about what one is and does and only secondarily, if at all, about how one looks.) Given these stereotypes, it is no wonder that beauty enjoys, at best, a rather mixed reputation.

It is not, of course, the desire to be beautiful that is wrong but the obligation to be—or to try. What is accepted by most women as a flattering idealization of their sex is a way of making women feel inferior to what they actually are—or normally grow to be. For the ideal of beauty is administered as a form of self-oppression. Women are taught to see their bodies in parts, and to evaluate each part separately. Breasts, feet, hips, waistline, neck, eyes, nose, complexion, hair, and so on—each in turn is submitted to an anxious, fretful, often despairing scrutiny. Even if some pass muster, some will always be found wanting. Nothing less than perfection will do.

In men, good looks is seen as a whole, something taken in at a glance. It does not need to be confirmed by giving measurements of different regions of the body, nobody encourages a man to dissect his appearance, feature by feature. As for perfection, that is considered trivial—almost unmanly. Indeed, in the ideally good-looking man a small imperfection or blemish is considered positively desirable. According to one movie critic (a woman) who is a declared Robert Redford fan, it is having that cluster of skin-colored moles on one cheek that saves Redford from being merely a "pretty face." Think of the depreciation of women—as well as of beauty—that is implied in that judgment.

"The privileges of beauty are immense," said Cocteau. To be sure, beauty is a form of power. And deservedly so. What is lamentable is that it is the only form of power that most women are encouraged to seek. This power is always conceived in relation to men; it is not the power to do but the power to attract. It is a power that negates itself. For this power is not one that can be chosen freely—at least, not by women—or renounced without social censure.

To preen, for a woman, can never be just a pleasure. It is also a duty. It is her work. If a woman does real work—and even if she has clambered up to a leading position in politics, law, medicine, business, or whatever—she is always under pressure to confess that she still works at being attractive. But in so far as she is keeping up as one of the fair sex, she brings under suspicion her very capacity to be objective, professional, authoritative, thoughtful. Damned if they do—woman are, and damned if they don't.

One could hardly ask for more important evidence of the dangers of considering persons as split between what is "inside" and what is "outside" than that interminable half-comic half-tragic tale, the oppression of women. How easy it is to start off by defining women as caretakers of their surfaces, and then to disparage them (or find them adorable) for being "superficial." It is a crude trap, and it has worked for too long. But to get out of the trap requires that women get some critical distance from that excellence and privilege which is beauty, enough distance to see how much beauty itself has been abridged in order to prop up the mythology of the "feminine." There should be a way of saving beauty *from* women—and *for* them.

# Reading for Detail

**Test your understanding of this text by filling gap in each blank or answer - ing the multiple-choice reading comprehension questions without looking back at the text. Choose the best answer from the choices listed.**

1. Greek people were assumed to be what we now have to call _________ persons.

ⓐ beautiful

ⓑ virtuous

ⓒ whole

2. We not only split off the "inside" from the "outside"; but we are actually surprised when someone who is beautiful is also _________, talented, good.

ⓐ handsome

ⓑ intelligent

ⓒ reserved

3. In every modern country that is Christian or post-Christian, women are the beautiful sex—to the detriment of the notion of _________ as well as of women.

ⓐ beauty

ⓑ excellence

ⓒ Christianity

4. It is not the desire to be beautiful that is wrong but the _________ to be—or to try.

ⓐ awareness

ⓑ obligation

ⓒ feminism

5. To be sure, beauty is a form of _________. And deservedly so.

ⓐ art

ⓑ immaturity

ⓒ power

6. Good looks does not need to be confirmed by giving measurements of different regions of the _________.

ⓐ body

ⓑ country

ⓒ world

7. If a woman does real work, she is always under pressure to confess that she still works at being _________.

ⓐ handsome

ⓑ essential

ⓒ attractive

8. How easy it is to start off by defining women as caretakers of their surfaces, and then to disparage them for being "_________."

ⓐ authoritative

ⓑ superficial

ⓒ feminine

## Comprehension Questions

**Read the text again and answer the following questions.**

1. What was the Greeks' idea about beauty? Explain it in two or three sentences.

2. What was the influence of Christianity on the definition of beauty?

3. In what countries can you call a man "beautiful"? And what's the difference between "beautiful" and "handsome"?

4. What is the difference in bodily perfection between men and women?

5. What does "being beautiful" mean to women?

Student No. : ______________________ Name : ______________________

# Expanding Vocabulary

**1** Each sentence contains an underlined word from the text, followed by three definitions. Put an √ next to the best meaning of the word as it is used in the sentence.

1. In fact, the instructor made adjustments in teaching style and <u>pedagogical</u> techniques after the first semester of teaching.

___ ⓐ educational

___ ⓑ too formal

___ ⓒ old-fashioned

2. The company provides child care <u>facilities</u>.

___ ⓐ conveniences

___ ⓑ equipments or buildings

___ ⓒ natural abilities

3. Music seemed to have lost its <u>enchantment</u> for her.

___ ⓐ magic spell

___ ⓑ mutual exchange

___ ⓒ being interested or attracted

4. He wanted to be free from the bondage of social <u>conventions</u>.

___ ⓐ traditional customs

___ ⓑ annual meetings

___ ⓒ community buildings

5. These seats are <u>reserved</u> for special guests.

___ ⓐ booked

___ ⓑ silent

___ ⓒ protected

6. The essence of his argument was that education should continue throughout life.

___ ⓐ small thing

___ ⓑ flavoring liquid

___ ⓒ important point

7. That colour doesn't suit your complexion.

___ ⓐ natural character

___ ⓑ skin color

___ ⓒ confusing aspect

8. She has an authoritative manner that at times is almost arrogant.

___ ⓐ commanding

___ ⓑ enigmatic

___ ⓒ authentic

## 2 Choose the best word to fill in the blank.

1. One of James Joyce's ________ had translated the poem.

ⓐ characteristics ⓑ talents

ⓒ attractions ⓓ disciples

2. He suffered a loss of ________ when the book didn't sell.

ⓐ narcissism ⓑ prestige

ⓒ feminism ⓓ identification

3. Boys are brainwashed into thinking that it's smart, trendy, and _______ to smoke.

ⓐ renounced ⓑ masculine

ⓒ pragmatic ⓓ complied

4. The exercise of patience is ________ in diplomatic negotiations.

ⓐ essential ⓑ tragic
ⓒ privileged ⓓ romantic

5. He may be wet behind the ears, but he's well trained and totally ________.

ⓐ superficial ⓑ competent
ⓒ disparaged ⓓ unmanly

6. She still showed ________ by the time she was twenty.

ⓐ reputation ⓑ detriment
ⓒ enchantment ⓓ immaturity

7. Several girls were ________ in front of the mirror.

ⓐ concocting ⓑ comprising
ⓒ preening ⓓ pivoting

8. It appears to be genuine, but I have my ________ about it.

ⓐ suspicion ⓑ complacence
ⓒ tranquility ⓓ reticence

9. It shows the name and picture of a person who suffered because of Nazi ________.

ⓐ suppression ⓑ oppression
ⓒ complexion ⓓ compression

10. U.S. officials acknowledge their reluctance to ________ the dollar's value.

ⓐ make up ⓑ come up with
ⓒ look down with ⓓ prop up

# Listen & Write

**Listen to the recorded text and write a two- or three-sentence summary.**

## 1

It was principally the influence of Christianity that deprived beauty of the central place it had in classical ideals of human excellence. By limiting excellence (virtus in Latin) to moral virtue only, Christianity set beauty adrift—as an alienated, arbitrary, superficial enchantment. And beauty has continued to lose prestige. For close to two centuries it has become a convention to attribute beauty to only one of the two sexes: the sex which, however fair, is always second. Associating beauty with women has put beauty even further on the defensive, morally.

---

## 2

It is not, of course, the desire to be beautiful that is wrong but the obligation to be—or to try. What is accepted by most women as a flattering idealization of their sex is a way of making women feel inferior to what they actually are—or normally grow to be. For the ideal of beauty is administered as a form of self-oppression. Women are taught to see their bodies in parts, and to evaluate each part separately. Breasts, feet, hips, waistline, neck, eyes, nose, complexion, hair, and so on—each in turn is submitted to an anxious, fretful, often despairing scrutiny. Even if some pass muster, some will always be found wanting. Nothing less than perfection will do.

---

## 3

"The privileges of beauty are immense," said Cocteau. To be sure, beauty is a form of power. And deservedly so. What is lamentable is that it is the only form of power that most women are encouraged to seek. This power is always conceived in relation to men; it is not the power to do but the power to attract. It is a power that negates itself. For this power is not one that can be chosen freely—at least, not by women—or renounced without social censure.

---

# Writing Assignment

Choose one of the following topics as your unit writing assignment.

1. Beauty for Man and Woman

2. The Privileges of Beauty

3. The Meaning of Being Beautiful

# As Good as New

When Tom Hatch's father died, Tom inherited a great deal of money. For a long time, he did not know what to spend it on, then one day he saw an advertisement for brains.

The advertisement said, "Get a better brain and lead a more successful life."

The advertisement had been put in the newspaper by a doctor. Tom went to see him.

"Please explain your advertisement to me," he said.

"Very well," the doctor answered. "Have you heard of heart transplants?"

"Yes," Tom said. "A heart transplant is when you take a heart from one person and put it into the body of another."

"That's correct," the doctor said. "Well, I do brain transplants. Now..." he pointed to a price list, "... we have several brains in stock. You can have a sanitation worker's brain for $5,000."

Tom shook his head.

"What about a university professor's brain? You can have one of those for $20,000," the doctor said.

This was interesting, Tom thought, but he wanted more information.

"Is that the most expensive brain?" he asked.

"No, you can have a judge's brain for $50,000," the doctor told him.

"That sounds very interesting," Tom said. "And is that the most expensive brain?"

The doctor shook his head. "Oh, no," he said. "The most expensive brain is a politician's. That will cost you $100,000."

Tom was surprised. "Why is a politician's brain so expensive?" he asked.

"Because it's never been used," the doctor said. "It's as good as new."

Unit 06

# The Student and the University

Look at the photos and think about the following questions.

1. What do you think is the role of the university in the modern world or in our society?

2. What is the most important thing for university students to do?

3. Do you enjoy college life? If no, why?

## Vocabulary Preview

**Here are some words and phrases from the reading. Put a check mark by the words you know. If you don' t know the meaning of a word, look it up in the dictionary.**

| | |
|---|---|
| ___ 1. intellectual | ___ 2. await |
| ___ 3. baccalaureate | ___ 4. sustain |
| ___ 5. traverse | ___ 6. alternative |
| ___ 7. overestimate | ___ 8. speculation |
| ___ 9. avoidance | ___ 10. philosophize |
| ___ 11. authoritarian | ___ 12. impose |
| ___ 13. vulgarity | ___ 14. discipline |
| ___ 15. distinctive | ___ 16. autochthonous |
| ___ 17. anarchy | ___ 18. legitimate |
| ___ 19. emerge | ___ 20. prescribe |
| ___ 21. curriculum | ___ 22. prospective |
| ___ 23. intimation | ___ 24. culminate |
| ___ 25. superiority | ___ 26. revelation |
| ___ 27. revitalize | ___ 28. gravity |
| ___ 29. confrontation | ___ 30. superficial |
| ___ 31. disruption | ___ 32. smorgasbord |
| ___ 33. sympathy | ___ 34. perversity |
| ___ 35. bewildering | ___ 36. immune |
| ___ 37. impediment | ___ 38. viable |
| ___ 39. demoralization | ___ 40. emancipate |
| ___ 41. navigate | ___ 42. sideshow |

## Skimming for Main Ideas

**Read the text one time quickly for the main ideas and put a check mark by the sentence that you think is mentioned in the reading text.**

___ a. The university now does not offer answers to students' questions about what courses they should take, what an educated human being is, or how they should study.

___ b. As soon as students become freshmen, they are guided by professors of the department who are assumed to have a great deal of knowledge about students' future career.

___ c. These days, college students are forced to experience a variety of departments and a variety of courses.

___ d. Fortunate students can find one or two professors who can give them insight into the great visions of education.

# Read

## The Student and the University: Liberal Education

What image does a first-rank college or university present today to a teen-ager leaving home for the first time, off to the adventure of a liberal education? He has four years of freedom to discover himself—a space between the intellectual wasteland he has left behind and the inevitable dreary professional training that awaits him after the baccalaureate. In this short time he must learn that there is a great world beyond the little one he knows, experience the exhilaration of it and digest enough of it to sustain himself in the intellectual deserts he is destined to traverse. He must do this, that is, if he is to have any hope of a higher life. These are the charmed years when he can, if he so chooses, become anything he wishes and when he has the opportunity to survey his alternatives, not merely those current in his time of provided by careers, but those available to him as a human being. The importance of these years for an American cannot be overestimated. They are civilization's only chance to get to him.

In looking at him we are forced to reflect on what he should learn if he is to be called educated; we must speculate on what the human potential to be fulfilled is. In the specialties we can avoid such speculation, and the avoidance of them is one of specialization's charms. But here it is a simple duty. What are we to teach this person? The answer may not be evident, but to attempt to answer the question is already to philosophize and to begin to educate. Such a concern in itself poses the question of the unity of man and the unity of the sciences. It is childishness to say, as some do, that everyone must be allowed to develop freely, that it is authoritarian to impose a point of view on the student. In that case, why have a university? If the response is "to provide an atmosphere for learning," we come back to our original questions at the second remove. Which atmosphere? Choices and reflection on the reasons for those choices are unavoidable. The university has to stand for something. The practical effects of unwillingness to think positively about the contents of a liberal education are, on the one hand, to ensure that all the vulgarities of the world outside the university will flourish within it, and on the other, to impose a much harsher and more illiberal necessity on the student—the one given by the imperial and imperious demands of the specialized disciplines unfiltered by unifying thought.

The university now offers no distinctive visage to the young person. He finds a democracy of the disciplines—which are there either because they are autochthonous or because they wandered in recently to perform some job that was demanded of the university. This democracy is really an anarchy, because there are no recognized rules for citizenship and no legitimate titles to rule. In short there is no vision, nor is there a set of competing visions, of what an educated human being is. The question has disappeared, for to pose it would be a threat to the peace. There is no organization of the sciences, no tree of knowledge. Out of chaos emerges dispiritedness, because it is impossible to make a reasonable choice. Better to give up on liberal education and get on with a specialty in which there is at least a prescribed curriculum and a prospective career. On the way the student can pick up in elective courses a little of whatever is thought to make one cultured. The student gets no intimation that great mysteries might be revealed to him, that new and higher motives of action might be discovered within him, that a different and more human way of life can be harmoniously constructed by what he is going to learn.

Simply, the university is not distinctive. Equality for us seems to culminate in the unwillingness and incapacity to make claims of superiority, particularly in the domains in which such claims have always been made—art, religion and philosophy. When Weber found that he could not choose between certain high opposites—reason vs. revelation, Buddha vs. Jesus—he did not conclude that all things are equally good, that the distinction between high and low disappears. As a matter of fact he intended to revitalize the consideration of these great alternatives in showing the gravity and danger involved in choosing among them; they were to be heightened in contrast to the trivial considerations of modern life that threatened to overgrow and render indistinguishable the profound problems the confrontation with which makes the bow of the soul taut. The serious intellectual life was for him the battleground of the great decisions, all of which are spiritual or "value"choices. One can no longer present this or that particular view of the educated or civilized man as authoritative; therefore one must say that education consists in knowing, really knowing, the small number of such views in their integrity. This distinction between profound and superficial—which takes the place of good and bad, true and false—provided a focus for serious study, but it hardly held out against the naturally relaxed democratic tendency to say, "Oh, what's the use?" The first university disruptions at Berkeley were explicitly directed against the multiversity smorgasbord and, I must confess, momentarily and partially engaged my sympathies. It may have even been the case that there was some small element of longing for an education in the motivation of those students. But nothing was done to guide to inform their energy, and the result was merely to add multilife-styles to multidisciplines, the diversity of perversity to the diversity of specialization. What we see so often happening in general happened here too; the insistent demand for greater community ended in greater isolation. Old agreement, old habit, old traditions were not so easily replaced.

Thus, when a student arrives at the university, he finds a bewildering variety of departments and a bewildering variety of courses. And there is no official guidance, no university-wide agreement, about what he should study. Nor does he usually find readily available examples, either among students or professors, of a unified use of the university's resources. It is easiest simply to make a career choice and go about getting prepared for that career. The programs designed for those having made such a choice render their students immune to charms that might lead them out of the conventionally respectable. The sirens sing sotto voce these days, and the young already have enough wax in their ears to pass them by without danger. These specialties can provide enough courses to take up most of their time for four years in preparation for the inevitable graduate study. With the few remaining course they can do what they please, taking a bit of this and a bit of that. No public career these days—not doctor nor lawyer nor politician nor journalist nor entertainer—has much to do with human learning. An education, other than purely professional or technical, can even seem to be an impediment. That is why a countervailing atmosphere in the university would be necessary for the students to gain a taste for intellectual pleasures and learn that they are viable.

The real problem is those students who come hoping to find out what career they want to have, or are simply looking for an adventure with themselves. There are plenty of things for them to do—courses and disciplines enough to spend many a lifetime on. Each department of great division of the university makes a pitch for itself, and each offers a course of study that will make the student an initiate. But how to choose among them? How do they relate to one another? The fact is they do not address one another. They are competing and contradictory, without being aware of it. The problem of the whole is urgently indicated by the very existence of the specialties, but it is never systematically posed. The net effect of the student's encounter with the college catalogue is bewilderment and very often demoralization. It is just a matter of chance whether he finds one or two professors who can give him an insight into one of the great visions of education that have been the distinguishing part of every civilized nation. Most professors are specialists, concerned only with their own fields, interested in the advancement of those fields in their own terms, or in their own personal advancement in a world where all the rewards are on the side of professional distinction. They have been entirely emancipated from the old structure of the university, which at least helped to indicate that they are incomplete, only parts of an unexamined and undiscovered whole. So the student must navigate among a collection of carnival barkers, each trying to lure him into a particular sideshow. This undecided student is an embarrassment to most universities, because he seems to be saying, "I am a whole human being. Help me to form myself in my wholeness and let me develop my real potential," and he is the one to whom they have nothing to say.

## Reading for Detail

**Test your understanding of this text by filling gap in each blank or answer - ing the multiple-choice reading comprehension questions without looking back at the text. Choose the best answer from the choices listed.**

1. What point does the author suggest for the university?

ⓐ The university is a place for students to find out his or her career.

ⓑ The university is a place for students to gain a taste for intellectual pleasures.

ⓒ The university is a place for students to get this or that particular view.

2. Why are universities important?

ⓐ Because it is a holy place to respect knowledge.

ⓑ Because it is the only chance for civilization to influence teenager.

ⓒ Because it is the only place for students to go when they to leave home.

3. What is the simple duty in looking at the first-come students?

ⓐ to speculate on what human potential to be fulfilled is

ⓑ to give the students a chance to meet the professors

ⓒ to answer the questions of the students

4. Why is the university really an anarchy?

ⓐ Because there are no leaders in the university.

ⓑ Because there are no students who respect professors.

ⓒ Because there are no recognized flues for citizenship and no legitimate titles to rule.

5. What does the education consist in knowing?

ⓐ the distinction between profound and superficial

ⓑ the distinction between reason and revelation

ⓒ the distinction between Buddha and Jesus

6. Why do the students-who come to university hoping to find out what career they want to have-face problems?

ⓐ Because they can find few professors to help them.

ⓑ Because they have many things to do enough courses and disciplines to spend many a lifetime on.

ⓒ Because they have too few things to do in order to achieve their goals in university.

7. Why can't the students get help from the professors?

ⓐ Because the students have their own insight into the fields of the education.

ⓑ Because the professors are competing and contradictory.

ⓒ Because the professors are concerned only with their own fields.

8. In what case is the student an embarrassment?

ⓐ In the case that the student is too bright.

ⓑ In the case that the student is too strong.

ⓒ In the case that the student is undecided.

## Comprehension Questions

**Read the text again and answer the following questions.**

1. What do the students have to learn during their university years?

2. Why is it childish to say that it is authoritarian to impose a point of view on the student in university?

3. What is the simplest and easiest way for university students to choose?

4. Why does the education of the nonprofessional or the nontechnical seem to be an impediment?

5. What do the students learn at university?

Student No. : ______________________ Name : ______________________

# Expanding Vocabulary

## 1 Each sentence contains an underlined word from the text, followed by three definitions. Put an √ next to the best meaning of the word as it is used in the sentence.

1. In this short time he must learn that there is a great world beyond the little one he knows, experience the <u>exhilaration</u> of it and digest enough of it to sustain himself in the intellectual deserts he is destined to traverse.

___ ⓐ amplification of something

___ ⓑ strong feeling of excitement

___ ⓒ particular way of behavior

2. These are the charmed years when he can, if he so chooses, become anything he wishes and when he has the opportunity to survey his <u>alternatives</u>, not merely those current in his time of provided by careers, but those available to him as a human being.

___ ⓐ other options

___ ⓑ rotation of two things

___ ⓒ replacement of something

3. The practical effects of unwillingness to think positively about the contents of a liberal education are, on the one hand, to ensure that all the <u>vulgarities</u> of the world outside the university will flourish within it,

___ ⓐ entering a building by force

___ ⓑ bad tastes or poor qualities

___ ⓒ main bad characters

4. This democracy is really an anarchy, because there are no recognized rules for citizenship and no <u>legitimate</u> titles to rule.

___ ⓐ enforced by law

___ ⓑ law-making

___ ⓒ reasonable and justified

5. Better to give up on liberal education and get on with a specialty in which there is at least a prescribed curriculum and a prospective career.

___ ⓐ anticipated

___ ⓑ progressing

___ ⓒ prosecuting

6. Equality for us seems to culminate in the unwillingness and incapacity to make claims of superiority, particularly in the domains in which such claims have always been made—art, religion and philosophy.

___ ⓐ happen suddenly

___ ⓑ cut in abruptly

___ ⓒ come to a head

7. When a student arrives at the university, he finds a bewildering variety of departments and a bewildering variety of courses.

___ ⓐ confusing

___ ⓑ careful

___ ⓒ fragrant

8. They have been entirely emancipated from the old structure of the university, which at least helped to indicate that they are incomplete, only parts of an unexamined and undiscovered whole.

___ ⓐ thin and weak

___ ⓑ liberated

___ ⓒ derived

## 2 Choose the best word to fill in the blank.

1. This new biography provides a fascinating account of the ________ of one of our most intrepid explorers.

ⓐ estimation ⓑ adventures
ⓒ wandering ⓓ career

2. This has led scientists to ________ on the existence of other galaxies.

ⓐ advance ⓑ avoid
ⓒ flourish ⓓ speculate

3. His tone of voice was so ________ that I wasn't sure if he was asking me for a loan or demanding payment of tribute.

ⓐ specialized ⓑ elective
ⓒ imperious ⓓ disrupted

4. With more research in specialized fields, following the progress in a particular ________ can be complicated.

ⓐ resource ⓑ discipline
ⓒ technology ⓓ community

5, His suicide attempt was the first ________ of how depressed he was.

ⓐ convention ⓑ sideshow
ⓒ isolation ⓓ intimation

6, Punishment varies according to the ________ of the offence.

ⓐ gravity ⓑ visage
ⓒ sympathy ⓓ variety

7. Officials warn of possible _________ to rail services over the holiday weekend.

ⓐ emancipation
ⓑ disruptions
ⓒ corruptions
ⓓ advancement

8. The press had criticized her so often that in the end she had become _________ to it.

ⓐ contradictory
ⓑ immune
ⓒ distinctive
ⓓ superficial

9. No matter how well qualified you may be, inability to get on well with other people will prove a serious _________ in any field of work.

ⓐ demoralization
ⓑ commitment
ⓒ specialization
ⓓ impediment

10. Sailors have special equipment to help them _________.

ⓐ organize
ⓑ navigate
ⓒ initiate
ⓓ revitalize

# Listen & Write

**Listen to the recorded text and write a two- or three-sentence summary.**

## 1

It is childishness to say, as some do, that everyone must be allowed to develop freely, that it is authoritarian to impose a point of view on the student. In that case, why have a university? If the response is "to provide an atmosphere for learning," we come back to our original questions at the second remove. Which atmosphere? Choices and reflection on the reasons for those choices are unavoidable. The university has to stand for something. The practical effects of unwillingness to think positively about the contents of a liberal education are, on the one hand, to ensure that all the vulgarities of the world outside the university will flourish within it, and on the other, to impose a much harsher and more illiberal necessity on the student—the one given by the imperial and imperious demands of the specialized disciplines unfiltered by unifying thought.

---

## 2

As a matter of fact he intended to revitalize the consideration of these great alternatives in showing the gravity and danger involved in choosing among them; they were to be heightened in contrast to the trivial considerations of modern life that threatened to overgrow and render indistinguishable the profound problems the confrontation with which makes the bow of the soul taut. The serious intellectual life was for him the battleground of the great decisions, all of which are spiritual or "value"choices. One can no longer present this or that particular view of the educated or civilized man as authoritative; therefore one must say that education consists in knowing, really knowing, the small number of such views in their integrity. This distinction between profound and superficial—which takes the place of good and bad, true and false—provided a focus for serious study, but it hardly held out against the naturally relaxed democratic tendency to say, "Oh, what's the use?"

---

## 3

The real problem is those students who come hoping to find out what career they want to have, or are simply looking for an adventure with themselves. There are plenty of things for them to do—courses and disciplines enough to spend many a lifetime on. Each department of great division of the university makes a pitch for itself, and each offers a course of study that will make the student an initiate. But how to choose among them? How do they relate to one another? The fact is they do not address one another. They are competing and contradictory, without being aware of it. The problem of the whole is urgently indicated by the very existence of the specialties, but it is never systematically posed.

---

# Writing Assignment

Choose one of the following topics as your unit writing assignment.

1. The University and Me

2. The Role of the University in Our Society

3. What We Should Learn in University

Unit 07

# The Fear of Change

**Look at the photos and think about the following questions.**

1. Think about the big changes that have happened for the past ten years. Which changes do you think are positive and which are negative?

2. Have you ever felt strains or tensions when you faced big changes? If so, why?

3. Do you know what cultural lag is? When do you think cultural lag occurs? What is the best solution to cultural lag?

## Vocabulary Preview

**Here are some words and phrases from the reading. Put a check mark by the words you know. If you don' t know the meaning of a word, look it up in the dictionary.**

| | | |
|---|---|---|
| ___ 1. lag | ___ 2. organize | ___ 3. supersonic |
| ___ 4. institution | ___ 5. loyalty | ___ 6. disparity |
| ___ 7. capitalism | ___ 8. strain | ___ 9. strive |
| ___ 10. corporation | ___ 11. adaptation | ___ 12. depositor |
| ___ 13. serenity | ___ 14. missionary | ___ 15. agitate |
| ___ 16. ailment | ___ 17. equitable | ___ 18. ignorance |
| ___ 19. territory | ___ 20. pigheaded | ___ 21. prerogative |
| ___ 22. adjustment | ___ 23. revolution | ___ 24. privilege |
| ___ 25. inertia | ___ 26. insoluble | ___ 27. precedence |
| ___ 28. slum | ___ 29. raid | ___ 30. evacuation |
| ___ 31. editorialist | ___ 32. emergency | ___ 33. contrive |

## Skimming for Main Ideas

**Read the text one time quickly for the main ideas and put a check mark by the sentence that you think is mentioned in the reading text.**

___ a. The most pressing problem of our world is the problem of technological advancement.

___ b. The rich and the wealthy resisted change mostly because of their fear.

___ c. Because of the war, institutions experienced change.

___ d. Ignorance, selfishness and a fear of losing prestige are the main reasons for cultural lag.

# Read

## The Fear of Change

The pressing problems of our world are the problems of cultural lag—problems arising from trying to organize a jet-propelled, supersonic, electronic, and atomic world with horse-and-buggy institutions. The rate of technological advancement for almost two hundred years now has been greater than the rate of the change of our social institutions and their accompanying loyalties and ideologies; and the disparity between the two rates is increasing rather than decreasing. Consequently, in every contemporary culture which has felt the impact of technology, people are questioning the appropriateness of nineteenth-century (eighteenth-century, medieval, or Stone Age) institutions to twentieth-century conditions. They are progressively more alarmed at the dangers arising from old-fashioned nationalism in a world that has become, technologically, one world; they are increasingly anxious over the possibility of attaining a sane world economic order with the instruments of nineteenth-century capitalism (or of nineteenth-century socialism). Whenever technologies are producing changes not adequately matched by changes in social institutions, there are people under strain and tension.

Some, of course, meet these strains and tensions and tensions in the only sensible way possible: they strive to change or abandon outmoded institutions and to bring into being new institutions or newer forms of old institutions. Changes in educational practice, in governmental organization, in the responsibilities of trade unions, in the structure of corporations, in the techniques of librarianship, in the marketing of agricultural commodities, and so on, go on all the time because people are constantly striving to bring institutions into closer relationship with reality. An especially successful example of institutional adaptation is the Federal

Deposit Insurance Corporation. Prior to 1934, bank failures resulted in the partial or total loss of the savings of depositors; panics, once started, were almost impossible to control. Since the setting up of FDIC, however, panics have disappeared. Bank failures are extremely rare, and even when they occur, depositors do not lose their money. American people now take the stability of their banks for granted, with a serenity that could hardly have been imagined before 1934. A more recent example of successful institutional adaptation in response to new problems is the Peace Corps—an ingenious combination of elements drawn from the military, the Civilian Conservation Corps of Depression days, the Salvation Army, and the missionary organizations of Christian churches. The common market is a triumphant example in Europe of what can be done by extensionally minded people when they are really determined to modify ancient social institutions and practices in favor of a more workable economic order.

Some people, however, seeing the need for changes, agitate for cures which, on examination, appear to be no better than the ailment; still others agitate for changes that cannot possibly be brought about. In some of the most important areas of human life—especially in our ideas about international relations and in the closely related problem of an equitable world economic order—areas in which our failure to find solutions threatens the future of civilization itself—we are, all over the world, in a state of cultural lag.

What causes this cultural lag? In the case of many groups, the cause is obviously ignorance. Some people manifestly don't know the score, so far as the realities of the modern world are concerned. Their "maps" represent "territories" that have long since passed out of existence. In other cases, the lag is due to fixed economic or political interests. Many individuals enjoy power and prestige within the framework of outmoded institutions-and with institutional inertia to support them, it is not hard for them to believe that their familiar institutions are beautiful and wonderful things. Indeed, there is little doubt that the desire of the wealthy and powerful to keep their wealth and power is a major reason for cultural lag in any society. Threatened with social change, they often act in such narrowly short-sighted and selfish ways that, like the Bourbons, they seem willing to destroy both the civilization they live in and themselves in grim, pigheaded attempts to hang on to their prerogatives.

But wealth and power are not in themselves guarantees either of social irresponsibility or of stupidity, and the existence of a powerful wealthy class in a culture is not in itself a guarantee that there will be cultural lag. At least some of the rich and powerful have known how to yield gracefully to institutional adjustments—sometimes they have even helped to introduce them—and by so doing they have maintained their favored position and have saved both society and themselves from the disasters that attend complete social disruption. When this happens, cultural lag is kept small enough to be manageable. In some Latin American countries today, there is a touch-and-go race going on between social reform and revolution, the outcome depending largely on the willingness of the privileged class to accept and adjust to change.

But even when the rich and powerful are shortsighted and irresponsible, they must have support among those who are neither rich nor powerful in order to be able to hold back necessary institutional adjustments. To comprehend cultural lag, we must account not only for the shortsightedness of the powerful but also for the shortsightedness of the ordinary citizen who supports policies that are contrary to his own interests. In addition to institutional inertia (which is a tremendous force for keeping people busy doing things they should have stopped doing long ago), it appears that fear is another major force influencing both rulers and the ruled in the direction of institutional rigidity. Perhaps the ultimate strength of cultural lag comes from those persons in all walks of life whom change has made afraid.

Whether the cultural lag arises from inertia, from shortsighted selfishness, form fear of change, or from a combination of these and other reasons, it is clear that the solution of social problems is basically a matter of adapting institutional habits to new conditions.

Perhaps the most dramatic thing about human behavior is how many problems which are "insoluble" for institution reasons are promptly solved the moment a war breaks out. War is an institution the demands of which, at least in modern culture, take precedence over almost all other demands. Before World War II, it would have been "impossible" to send the slum children of London to the country for the sake of their health. But when the air raids on London began, the evacuation of all the children took place over a weekend. Institutionally minded men, before the war, demonstrated time and again that it was "impossible" for either Germany or Japan to fight without an adequate gold supply. Nevertheless, Germany and Japan did manage to put up quite a fight according to editorialists and economists. At Sydenham, England and at Biarritz, France, the American government put together, almost overnight after the war closed, two great universities for GI's in Europe. Textbooks and equipment were flown over, luxurious quarters were provided for the thousands of students, and distinguished professors from the leading universities of America were hired at handsome salaries in order to provide, for a very short time, an educational Utopia for war-wearied American soldiers. In ordinary times, is there any conceivable way in which a similar university could be set up, say, in Mississippi, the state which, since it has the least per capita to spend on education, would be in greatest need of such a school? One of the lessons of war is that institutions, while powerful and long-lasting, are often not insuperably rigid if the emergency is great enough.

The problem, then, the world over, is to learn that the emergency is serious enough—in international affairs, in race relations, in the world population explosion, and in many other areas—to require modifying or abandoning some of our institutions. And the problem for us as citizens, once we understand the emergency, is how we can contrive ways of adjusting our thinking and acting so that institutional adjustments may be made both realistically and rapidly, with a minimum of human suffering and a maximum of general benefit.

## Reading for Detail

**Test your understanding of this text by filling gap in each blank or answer - ing the multiple-choice reading comprehension questions without looking back at the text. Choose the best answer from the choices listed.**

1. What is the most pressing problem of our world?

ⓐ the problem of technological advancement
ⓑ the problem of ideology
ⓒ the problem of cultural lag

2. What causes the changes in institutions?

ⓐ the desire to meet the strains and tensions
ⓑ the striving to control the panics
ⓒ the striving to bring institutions into closer relationship with reality

3. What has been the usual response of the wealthy and the powerful to the social changes?

ⓐ to yield gracefully to institutional adjustments
ⓑ to give willingly the wealth and power to the poor
ⓒ to keep their wealth and power

4. Since when do the depositors not lose their money?

ⓐ since the setting up of Federal Deposit Insurance Corporation
ⓑ since the establishment of the Salvation Army
ⓒ since the setting up of the Peace-Corps

5. What is a major reason for cultural lag in any society?

ⓐ the desire of the wealthy and powerful to keep their wealth and power
ⓑ the desire of the wealthy and powerful to yield gracefully to institutional adjustments
ⓒ the desire of the wealthy and powerful to accept and adjust to change

6. With the institutional inertia what is influencing in the direction of institutional rigidity?

ⓐ the desire of the powerful

ⓑ the desire of the wealthy

ⓒ the fear of the rulers and the ruled

7. Why do you think the war is the most dramatic event in human history?

ⓐ Because people fight without any cause.

ⓑ Because it solves many insoluble problems.

ⓒ Because it gives health to the children.

8. In what case could the university be set up in a desert almost overnight?

ⓐ in a case of war

ⓑ in a case of business

ⓒ in a case of general education

## Comprehension Questions

**Read the text again and answer the following questions.**

1. What are the causes of cultural lag?

2. How do people meet the strains and tensions arising from cultural lag?

3. What is the common act of the rich and powerful in the face of social changes?

4. In what case is cultural lag kept small enough to be manageable?

5. What is the lesson of war?

Student No. : ____________________ Name : ____________________

# Expanding Vocabulary

## 1 Each sentence contains an underlined word from the text, followed by three definitions. Put an √ next to the best meaning of the word as it is used in the sentence.

1. The pressing problems of our world are the problems of cultural lag.

___ ⓐ delay

___ ⓑ lack

___ ⓒ difference

2. Whenever technologies are producing changes not adequately matched by changes in social institutions, there are people under strain and tension.

___ ⓐ calm and relaxed state

___ ⓑ time indication of present or past

___ ⓒ a feeling of worry and anxiety

3. An especially successful example of institutional adaptation is the Federal Deposit Insurance Corporation.

___ ⓐ application

___ ⓑ conversion

___ ⓒ fostering

4. American people now take the stability of their banks for granted, with a serenity that could hardly have been imagined before 1934.

___ ⓐ steadiness

___ ⓑ disruption

___ ⓒ familiarization

5. Some people, however, seeing the need for changes, agitate for cures which, on examination, appear to be no better than the ailment.

___ ⓐ protest to get something

___ ⓑ think clearly or calmly

___ ⓒ perform successfully

6. Threatened with social change, they often act in such narrowly short-sighted and selfish ways that, like the Bourbons, they seem wiling to destroy both the civilization they live in and themselves in grim, pigheaded attempts to hang on to their prerogatives.

___ ⓐ immaturity

___ ⓑ precedence

___ ⓒ privilege

7. In addition to institutional inertia, it appears that fear is another major force influencing both rulers and the ruled in the direction of institutional rigidity.

___ ⓐ being unavoidable

___ ⓑ tendency to remain still

___ ⓒ being unfavored by someone

8. But when the air raids on London began, the evacuation of all the children took place over a weekend.

___ ⓐ avoidance of meeting

___ ⓑ sending to a hospital

___ ⓒ sending to a safe place

## 2 Choose the best word to fill in the blank.

1. Her colleagues paid tribute to her outstanding ________ and commitment to the firm.

   ⓐ royalty　　ⓑ apprehension
   ⓒ proclamation　　ⓓ loyalty

2. ________ is also based upon the free exchange of goods and services in the world market.

   ⓐ Nationalism　　ⓑ Commercialism
   ⓒ Capitalism　　ⓓ Pragmatism

3. I don't think free enterprise can really be free if it's dominated by a few giant ________ or monopolies.

   ⓐ governments　　ⓑ individuals
   ⓒ corporations　　ⓓ fundamentals

4. Today's world is running low on ________ but high on strains and stress.

   ⓐ serenity　　ⓑ continuity
   ⓒ strife　　ⓓ suspension

5. The ________ went to Africa to convert people to Christianity.

   ⓐ editorialist　　ⓑ raider
   ⓒ missionary　　ⓓ ideologist

6. Forgive my ________, but what exactly are you talking about?

   ⓐ equitability　　ⓑ ignorance
   ⓒ shortsightedness　　ⓓ disparity

7. Almost every Western nation has had its era of ________ or civil war.

   ⓐ revolution　　ⓑ slums
   ⓒ civilization　　ⓓ agriculture

8. Some people think that fluency and communication take ________ over grammar when speaking.

ⓐ precedence ⓑ strain
ⓒ adjustment ⓓ equipment

9. In an early morning ________ on the hotel, federal agents handcuffed him.

ⓐ ailment ⓑ rigidity
ⓒ raid ⓓ adequacy

10. South Korea has called an ________ meeting of top cabinet officials.

ⓐ emergent ⓑ benefit
ⓒ sensible ⓓ emergency

# Listen & Write

**Listen to the recorded text and write a two- or three-sentence summary.**

## 1

The pressing problems of our world are the problems of cultural lag—problems arising from trying to organize a jet-propelled, supersonic, electronic, and atomic world with horse-and-buggy institutions. The rate of technological advancement for almost two hundred years now has been greater than the rate of the change of our social institutions and their accompanying loyalties and ideologies; and the disparity between the two rates is increasing rather than decreasing. Consequently, in every contemporary culture which has felt the impact of technology, people are questioning the appropriateness of nineteenth-century (eighteenth-century, medieval, or Stone Age) institutions to twentieth-century conditions.

## 2

What causes this cultural lag? In the case of many groups, the cause is obviously ignorance. Some people manifestly don't know the score, so far as the realities of the modern world are concerned. Their "maps" represent "territories" that have long since passed out of existence. In other cases, the lag is due to fixed economic or political interests. Many individuals enjoy power and prestige within the framework of outmoded institutions-and with institutional inertia to support them, it is not hard for them to believe that their familiar institutions are beautiful and wonderful things. Indeed, there is little doubt that the desire of the wealthy and powerful to keep their wealth and power is a major reason for cultural lag in any society.

## 3

But even when the rich and powerful are shortsighted and irresponsible, they must have support among those who are neither rich nor powerful in order to be able to hold back necessary institutional adjustments, To comprehend cultural lag, then, we must account not only for the shortsightedness of the powerful but also for the shortsightedness of the ordinary citizen who supports policies that are contrary to his own interests. In addition to institutional inertia (which is a tremendous force for keeping people busy doing things they should have stopped doing ling ago), it appears that fear is another major force influencing both rulers and the ruled in the direction of institutional rigidity. Perhaps the ultimate strength of cultural lag comes form those persons in all walks of life whom change has made afraid.

# Writing Assignment

Choose one of the following topics as your unit writing assignment.

1. The Cause of Cultural Lag

2. Institutional Inertia and the War

3. How to Face the Rapidly Changing World

Unit 08

# Napoleon Enters Moscow

Look at the photos and think about the following questions.

1. What do you know about Napoleon? What do you think of him?

2. When you read the title, 'Napoleon Enters Moscow,' what images or pictures came to mind?

3. Why do we call Napoleon a hero? What other names might you call him?

## Vocabulary Preview

Here are some words and phrases from the reading. Put a check mark by the words you know. If you don' t know the meaning of a word, look it up in the dictionary.

| | |
|---|---|
| ___ 1. retreat | ___ 2. premature |
| ___ 3. cupola | ___ 4. lull |
| ___ 5. inhabitant | ___ 6. implore |
| ___ 7. menace | ___ 8. tumult |
| ___ 9. solitude | ___ 10. artillery |
| ___ 11. habitation | ___ 12. aristocracy |
| ___ 13. citadel | ___ 14. imperial |
| ___ 15. sovereign | ___ 16. sanctuary |
| ___ 17. surmount | ___ 18. enchase |
| ___ 19. extinguish | ___ 20. conflagration |
| ___ 21. furnace | ___ 22. devour |
| ___ 23. intact | ___ 24. mingle |
| ___ 25. inflammable | ___ 26. sinister |
| ___ 27. wretched | ___ 28. pillage |
| ___ 29. labyrinth | ___ 30. stupor |

## Skimming for Main Ideas

Read the text one time quickly for the main ideas and put a check mark by the sentence that you think is mentioned in the reading text.

___ a. Only noblemen in Moscow welcomed Napoleon when he entered the city.

___ b. When Napoleon entered Moscow, there occurred tumult which disturbed the solitude of the city.

___ c. As soon as Napoleon entered the Kremlin, a big fire broke out in Moscow.

___ d. The big fire was extinguished soon by the French soldiers.

# Read

## Napoleon Enters Moscow, 14 September 1812

Baron Claude François de Méneval

*Retreating before Napoleon the Russians under Kutuzov adopted a scorched-earth policy, abandoning Moscow, which Napoleon entered unopposed. The premature onset of winter made his subsequent withdrawal from Moscow disastrous.*

A curious and impressive sight was this sudden appearance of this great city, Asiatic rather than European, spreading out at the end of a desert and naked plain, topped with its twelve hundred spires and sky-blue cupolas, strewn with golden stars, and linked one to the other with gilded chains. This conquest had been dearly paid for, but Napoleon at that time lulled himself in the hope that he would be able to dictate peace there. The King of Naples, who entered it first, sent word to the Emperor that the city appeared to be deserted and that no civil or military functionary, nor nobleman, nor priest had presented himself. The Russian army had taken away the majority of the inhabitants of Moscow in its train. Some Russian and foreign dealers, who had managed to escape this order, came to see the Emperor and implored him to protect them against the pillaging with which they thought themselves menaced. There had remained in the city only a few thousand people belonging to the lowest classes of society, who had nothing to lose by awaiting the course of events.

Napoleon passed this night of September 14th in the Dorogomilow *faubourg*, and only entered Moscow on the morrow. The entry was not accompanied by that tumult which marks the taking possession of a great city. No noise disturbed the solitude of the city streets, save only the rumbling of the cannon and of the artillery *caissons*. Moscow seemed asleep in deep sleep, like one of those enchanted cities of which we read in Arabian tales. The streets through which we passed were lined with houses of fine appearance for the most part, with closed windows and doors. Palaces with colonnades, churches and beautiful buildings glittering with the luxury of Europe and of Asia raised themselves side by side with very modest habitations. All bespoke the ease and wealth of a great city enriched by trade and inhabited by a wealthy and numerous aristocracy. Some of the principal houses which we were able to enter were well appointed and well furnished, many even magnificently so, and their inhabitants did not appear to have abandoned them for ever.

The Emperor proceeded directly to the Kremlin, a large citadel placed in the centre of the town, on the top of a hill, surrounded with an embattled wall and flanked at intervals with towers armed with cannon. The Kremlin is a second city. It contains the imperial palace, the arsenal, the Senate palace, the archives, the principal public establishments, a large number of churches, temples filled with historical curiosities, objects serving for the coronation of the sovereigns, and lastly trophies and flags taken from the Turks. It is in one of the principal temples that are the tombs of the Tsars. In this imposing *fane* reigns a magnificence which is half barbaric and of a primitive character. The walls are covered with thick plates of gold and silver on which are figured in relief the principal incidents of the Sacred History. Enormous silver lamps of Byzantine shape hang from the arches of the building, large many-branched chandeliers of the same metal stand on pedestals on the floor. There is also to be seen in this sanctuary a portrait of the Holy Virgin attributed to St. Luke, the frame of this picture is enriched with pearls and precious stones. A great bell-tower, known as the Ivan tower, was surmounted by a gigantic cross in the centre of which was enchased a cross of pure gold containing a fragment of the true cross. This cross and a number of curious objects which could be removed were to be sent to Paris from the Kremlin.

Hardly had the Emperor entered the Kremlin than fire broke out in the Kitaigorod, or Chinese city, an immense bazaar, surrounded by porticoes, in which were heaped up, in large shops or in cellars, the entrances to which were placed in the middle of the streets, precious goods of every kind, such as shawls, furs, Indian and Chinese tissues. Fruitless efforts were made to extinguish the flames, and the burning of the bazaar became the signal for a general conflagration in the city. This conflagration, spreading rapidly, devoured three-quarters of Moscow in three days. Each moment one saw smoke followed by flames breaking out of houses which had remained intact and in the end the fire broke out in every house in the city. The town was one mighty furnace from which sheaves of fire burst heavenwards lighting up the horizon with the glaring flames and spreading a burning heat. These masses of flame, mingling together, were rapidly caught up by a strong wind which spread them in every direction. They were accompanied by a succession of whistling noises and explosions caused by the falling walls and the explosion of inflammable materials which were stored in the shops and houses. To these roaring noises, to these sinister outbreaks added themselves the cries and yells of the wretched people who were caught by the flames in the houses which they had entered to pillage and which many escaped only to perish in the streets which formed a blazing labyrinth from which all escape was impossible. Motionless and in the silence of stupor we looked on at this horrible and magnificent spectacle, with the feeling of our absolute helplessness to render any assistance.

## Reading for Detail

**Test your understanding of this text by filling gap in each blank or answering the multiple-choice reading comprehension questions without looking back at the text. Choose the best answer from the choices listed.**

1. What did Napoleon find when he entered Moscow?

___ ⓐ an army

___ ⓑ noblemen and priests

___ ⓒ people of lowest classes

2. When did Napoleon enter Moscow?

___ ⓐ spring

___ ⓑ summer

___ ⓒ winter

3. What happened to Kremlin upon Napoleon's arrival?

___ ⓐ People welcomed him.

___ ⓑ Fire broke out.

___ ⓒ Armed soldiers attacked him.

4. Many people in Kremlin died because of what?

___ ⓐ conflagration

___ ⓑ bomb

___ ⓒ starvation

## Comprehension Questions

**Read the text again and answer the following questions.**

1. How did Napoleon think of the prospect of conquering Moscow?

2. How was the appearance of Moscow when Napoleon entered it?

3. Describe briefly how the Kremlin looked like?

4. How did people respond to the fire in the Kremlin?

Student No. : ____________________ Name : ____________________

# Expanding Vocabulary

## 1 Each sentence contains an underlined word from the text, followed by three definitions. Put an √ next to the best meaning of the word as it is used in the sentence.

1. Napoleon at that time lulled himself in the hope that he would be able to dictate peace there.

___ ⓐ soothed ___ ⓑ sang ___ ⓒ tried

2. The entry was not accompanied by that tumult which marks the taking possession of a great city.

___ ⓐ confusion ___ ⓑ reception ___ ⓒ silence

3. Moscow seemed like an enchanted city.

___ ⓐ enclosed ___ ⓑ besieged ___ ⓒ bewitched

4. The inhabitants did not appear to have abandoned them for ever.

___ ⓐ inhabited ___ ⓑ forsaken ___ ⓒ banned

5. There is also to be seen in this sanctuary a portrait of the Holy Virgin.

___ ⓐ temple ___ ⓑ sanction ___ ⓒ saloon

6. The burning of the bazaar became the signal for a general conflagration.

___ ⓐ fire ___ ⓑ tumult ___ ⓒ noise

7. To these sinister outbreaks added themselves the cries of the wretched people.

___ ⓐ cold ___ ⓑ evil ___ ⓒ sudden

8. In the silence of stupor we looked on at this spectacle.

___ ⓐ bewilderment ___ ⓑ stupidity ___ ⓒ wonder

## 2 Choose the best word to fill in the blank.

1. Don't be ________ into thinking that because you've explained it, the school taught it, or your child saw it on TV, he really got it.

   ⓐ lulled ⓑ mad ⓒ silly ⓓ foolish

2. People commonly travel the world over to see rivers and mountains, new stars, freak fish, grotesque breeds of human; they fall into an animal _______ that gapes at existence and they think they have seen something.

   ⓐ agitation ⓑ activity ⓒ wisdom ⓓ stupor

3. Life is not so _________, grave. Matter of fact has made them brave.

   ⓐ charming ⓑ sinister ⓒ sudden ⓓ bewildered

4. Children belong in families, which, ideally, serve as a(n) _________ and a cushion from the world at large

   ⓐ sanctuary ⓑ example ⓒ prison ⓓ school

5. New York is full of _________ churches. A Godless city, but full of superstitions on every subject-art, money, sex, food, health.

   ⓐ faithful ⓑ enchanted ⓒ amazing ⓓ abandoned

6. We must never confuse elegance with _________.

   ⓐ stupor ⓑ sanctuary ⓒ snobbery ⓓ transparence

7. All beauties contain, like all possible phenomena, something eternal and something _________, something absolute and something particular.

   ⓐ transitory ⓑ transcendent ⓒ minute ⓓ simultaneous

# Listen & Write

**Listen to the recorded text and write a two- or three-sentence summary.**

## 1

A curious and impressive sight was this sudden appearance of this great city, Asiatic rather than European, spreading out at the end of a desert and naked plain, topped with its twelve hundred spires and sky-blue cupolas, strewn with golden stars, and linked one to the other with gilded chains. This conquest had been dearly paid for, but Napoleon at that time lulled himself in the hope that he would be able to dictate peace there. The King of Naples, who entered it first, sent word to the Emperor that the city appeared to be deserted and that no civil or military functionary, nor nobleman, nor priest had presented himself.

## 2

The Emperor proceeded directly to the Kremlin, a large citadel placed in the centre of the town, on the top of a hill, surrounded with an embattled wall and flanked at intervals with towers armed with cannon. The Kremlin is a second city. It contains the imperial palace, the arsenal, the Senate palace, the archives, the principal public establishments, a large number of churches, temples filled with historical curiosities, objects serving for the coronation of the sovereigns, and lastly trophies and flags taken from the Turks. It is in one of the principal temples that are the tombs of the Tsars. In this imposing fane reigns a magnificence which is half barbaric and of a primitive character. The walls are covered with thick plates of gold and silver on which are figured in relief the principal incidents of the Sacred History.

## 3

Hardly had the Emperor entered the Kremlin than fire broke out in the Kitaigorod, or Chinese city, an immense bazaar, surrounded by porticoes, in which were heaped up, in large shops or in cellars, the entrances to which were placed in the middle of the streets, precious goods of every kind, such as shawls, furs, Indian and Chinese tissues. Fruitless efforts were made to extinguish the flames, and the burning of the bazaar became the signal for a general conflagration in the city. This conflagration, spreading rapidly, devoured three-quarters of Moscow in three days. Each moment one saw smoke followed by flames breaking out of houses which had remained intact and in the end the fire broke out in every house in the city.

# Writing Assignment

Choose one of the following topics as your unit writing assignment.

1. Napoleon's Withdrawal from Moscow

2. Napoleon: Hero or Villain?

3. Do you want to live a life like Napoleon?

Unit 09

# A Fish Story

Look at the photos and think about the following questions.

1. What do you see in the photo? Where do you think they are?

2. Have you been there? If so, what was your favorite place in the park? If not, do you want to visit the park sometime later?

3. List three places you want to visit in the future. Why do you want to go there and what do you want to see there?

## Vocabulary Preview

**Here are some words and phrases from the reading. Put a check mark by the words you know. If you don' t know the meaning of a word, look it up in the dictionary.**

| | | |
|---|---|---|
| ___ 1. superlative | ___ 2. achievement | ___ 3. geyser |
| ___ 4. thermal | ___ 5. extinct | ___ 6. bison |
| ___ 7. acclaim | ___ 8. sanctuary | ___ 9. genetically |
| ___ 10. fare | ___ 11. isolate | ___ 12. slash |
| ___ 13. gill | ___ 14. decline | ___ 15. imperil |
| ___ 16. stronghold | ___ 17. intact | ___ 18. ecological |
| ___ 19. collapse | ___ 20. angle | ___ 21. spawn |
| ___ 22. predator | ___ 23. hibernation | ___ 24. replenish |
| ___ 25. recoup | ___ 26. voracious | ___ 27. thaw |
| ___ 28. immune | ___ 29. clandestinely | ___ 30. invulnerable |
| ___ 31. ramification | ___ 32. garner | |

## Skimming for Main Ideas

**Read the text one time quickly for the main ideas and put a check mark by the sentence that you think is mentioned in the reading text.**

___ a. Yellowstone National Park has played an important role in the protection of the genetically pure Yellowstone cutthroat trout.

___ b. The yellowstone cutthroat is regarded as evidence which shows that the park is well developed for anglers.

___ c. Lake trouts caught in Yellowstone Lake were regarded as a symbol of success in conservation of nature.

___ d. Where lake trout are concentrated, the number of cutthroat trout has declined.

# Read

## A Fish Story

Yellowstone National Park is well known for many superlatives and achievements: first national park in the world; home to the largest number of geysers and thermal features on the planet; site of the first successful effort to save a nearly extinct species (the bison); and acclaimed for possessing all of the native species it had when the park was established more than 125 years ago. A lesser-known yet extremely significant accomplishment is the national park's role as a sanctuary for the genetically pure Yellowstone cutthroat trout.

In the Western United States, where native fish have not fared well, the Yellowstone cutthroat is in better shape than most. This comparative advantage exists largely because the heart of its range overlaps Yellowstone, where years of protection have isolated the fish from many problems faced by other native cutthroat subspecies.

Named for the red slash on its gills, the cutthroat is one of the most beautiful trout in the world, typically a golden hue with black spots and pinkish-rose sides and throat. This fish once had the widest geographic distribution of any native trout in the West, with 14 subspecies ranging from New Mexico to Alberta and from the Rockies to the Pacific Northwest and southeast Alaska. Despite this huge geographical range, the cutthroat as a species has not fared well: Two subspecies are extinct, ten have suffered steep declines, and only two are thought to be holding their own.

Like other subspecies of cutthroat trout, the Yellowstone cutthroat has declined in numbers across its geographic range. The Montana Department of Fish, Wildlife, and Parks has designated it a "species of concern," meaning that the department considers its future in the state imperiled. Even in Yellowstone, the fish's stronghold, "Only 10 percent of the original stock of genetically pure stream-inhabiting

Yellowstone cutthroat trout are still intact today," says Yellowstone National Park fishery biologist Jim Ruzycki.

Nevertheless, according to Ruzycki, Yellowstone Lake is the last large lake in the West with healthy native cutthroat trout populations. The fish is now a key part of the park's ecological balance.

In the first half of the 20th century, human activities put cutthroat populations in Yellowstone National Park at risk. Commercial fishing (catching fish to feed tourists) and sport fishing removed millions of large trout. Although commercial fishing ended in 1917, aggressive individual fishing continued, so that by the 1960s, Yellowstone Lake's trout fishery had collapsed. In response, the Park Service adopted new regulations in 1975, requiring anglers to return unharmed to the lake all trout larger than 13 inches.

These new regulations, designed to protect spawning-age fish stock, worked better than anyone had imagined. As a result, the lake's cutthroat population underwent a major turn-around, and trout size and numbers increased dramatically. Within a decade, people were again catching dozens of fish a day—nearly all of them larger than 13 inches—and throwing them back. Unlike other cutthroat populations, the future of the Yellowstone subspecies appeared assured.

But happy anglers were not the only consequence. Where spawning runs had previously dwindled to a trickle of fish, thousands of adult Yellowstone cutthroat trout averaging 16 to 20 inches long now jammed the more than 100 spawning streams that enter Yellowstone Lake. As the trout recovery continued, animals from bald eagles to river otters began to use the spawning streams as a food source.

To biologists, the most exciting effect of the growing trout population was the increasing consumption of spawning trout by the park's largest predator—the grizzly bear. "On the good fishable spawning streams, bears can capture a lot of energy efficiently," says grizzly bear management biologist Kerry Gunther. "I watched one bear catch 20 trout in a half hour", Gunther says. "The fish provide grizzlies with one of the highest energy sources per kilogram of food of any resource in the park." The timing of the spawning run from late May through June is another reason the cutthroat trout is so valuable to bears. At that time of year, grizzlies have just come out of hibernation and need to replenish their energy supplies, but there's not a lot of other food around. Dan Reinhart, management biologist for the Lake District, affirms that "trout are an early season food that helps bears recoup hibernation losses." And it's not just grizzlies that benefit. Gunther says he has seen black bears, mink, otter, and coyotes fishing in the spawning streams—and perhaps even wolves may benefit.

By the early 1980s, the restoration of Yellowstone Lake's cutthroat fishery was hailed as a major conservation success story. But the cheering stopped in the summer of 1994, when rangers were presented with a lake trout by an angler who claimed it was taken from Yellowstone Lake. Park officials were dumbfounded. Lake trout are voracious predators of the cutthroat and were not supposed to be in Yellowstone Lake at all. A few days later a second lake trout was caught and reported. Fearing the worst, park officials set gill nets in the lake and immediately captured a few more.

The undisputed presence of those fish prompted park officials to go back and check angling record cards, which all fishers in Yellowstone turn in when they leave. What they found was not reassuring. It turned out that anglers had reported catching lake trout from Yellowstone Lake every now and then for ten years or so. However, none of the fish was brought in for verification, and officials had assumed lake trout reports were the result of misidentification by inexperienced anglers.

How long lake trout have been in Yellowstone Lake isn't known for certain. According to Stu Coleman, chief of Yellowstone's natural resources branch, the trout were probably introduced between 30 and 50 years ago. As Coleman explains, "The fish don't mature until they are five years of age, and we have taken some fish that are 18 to 20 years old. They are likely the offspring of fish that were originally introduced."

The fact that few lake trout were caught all these years isn't difficult to explain.

Lake trout prefer very cold water, so they appear in shallow water only just after the ice thaws in the spring and just before the lake freezes in the fall. Fishing is closed in the lake during both of these seasons. During the summer, when fishing season is open and the lake is accessible to anglers, lake trout are usually found in waters 50 to 100 feet deep, far below the average depth most people fish.

Exactly how lake trout got into Yellowstone Lake remains a mystery. The fish is not native to the Yellowstone area or even to the West. Its natural range includes most of the northern-tier states from Maine to Minnesota and across Canada into Alaska. Lake trout found in the western United States south of Glacier National Park are almost exclusively the result of introductions.

In the past, stocking exotic fish to improve angling was standard practice for natural resource agencies. Like an army of aquatic Johnny Appleseeds, government employees and private individuals planted non-native fish willy-nilly across the landscape without regard to existing fish populations or the biological consequences. Yellowstone was not immune to this practice. Non-native fish including brook, brown, and rainbow trout were all successfully introduced into some Yellowstone waters. However, there is no record of lake trout being introduced into the lake by the Park Service or anyone else. The most plausible explanation for their presence is that an angler clandestinely planted them there once in a mistaken—not to mention illegal—attempt to improve fishing.

The damage caused by lake trout extends beyond the desire for ecosystem purity. Lake trout are voracious predators, and they grow quite large. Commercial fishermen in the Great Lakes have caught lake trout of up to 100 pounds. By the time they are about 13 inches long, they begin to feed heavily on other fish. Since Yellowstone Lake has just a few species of fish, the only real prey for lake trout are cutthroats. Fishery biologist Jim Ruzycki says a mature 30-inch lake trout will eat about 90 cutthroats a year: "Since they can eat fish up to half of their body length, there aren't many cuts invulnerable to this."

Whether the lake trout are already affecting the population of cutthroat trout is open to some debate. "We've seen lower numbers of spawning fish in streams for the past few years," says Gunther. "Yet, this past year, spawning fish numbers have gone up, except for the West Thumb area, where lake trout are concentrated." While it is tempting to blame the lake trout for these declines, there may be a number of other factors at work. For instance, a serious drought in the early 1990s could have affected fish populations.

If left uncontrolled, however, lake trout could come to dominate Yellowstone Lake, which biologists speculate will have significant ramifications for both cutthroat and Yellowstone's other wildlife. Unlike cutthroats trout, lake trout spawn in deep water in the fall, so they are unavailable as a food source to most of the park's wildlife.

The animal garnering the most concern is the park's grizzly bears. Yellowstone National Park's grizzlies have a limited menu of potential food sources compared with other bear populations. Wipe out the trout, and the survival of the entire Greater Yellowstone grizzly bear population may be in jeopardy. In a study done in the early 1990s, Dan Reinhart estimated 44 different bears were eating from spawning streams. This number may represent one-fifth of all grizzlies in the Greater Yellowstone ecosystem.

The Park Service is not waiting to see whether lake trout create a problem; it is hoping to halt the problem before it gets worse. One way to reduce lake trout recruitment is gill netting the fish on their spawning beds. "It turns out that lake trout have a real fidelity to certain spawning grounds," says Yellowstone's Coleman. "They usually spawn in ten to 30 feet of water over rocky bottoms."

The park may now face a never-ending program of lake trout control, and containing lake trout numbers is expensive. According to Stu Coleman, 65 percent of the park's fishery budget is now focused on lake trout. "For every dollar we put on trying to solve this problem, that's a dollar we can't put somewhere else," he says. But the cost of not doing so threatens a world-renowned biological resource — the last large viable population of Yellowstone cutthroat trout in the world. That is a cost that many in and out of the Park Service feel is too high.

# Reading for Detail

**Test your understanding of this text by filling gap in each blank or answer - ing the multiple-choice reading comprehension questions without looking back at the text. Choose the best answer from the choices listed.**

1. Yellowstone National Park is the only place where we can find the ________, which is extinct in other areas of the United States.

ⓐ bison

ⓑ dinosaur

ⓒ otter

2. A long time ago, ________ subspecies of the cutthroat ranged from New Mexico to Alberta and from the Rockies to the Pacific Northweat and southeast Alaska.

ⓐ ten

ⓑ twelve

ⓒ fourteen

3. In the early 20th century, ________ fishing and sport fishing caused a sharp decline in the number of the cutthroat trout in the park.

ⓐ commercial

ⓑ organized

ⓒ military

4. New regulations in 1970s required anglers not to catch any trout larger than ________ inches.

ⓐ 10

ⓑ 13

ⓒ 16

5. The cheering of the successful restoration of the park's cutthroat fishery stopped because _________ was found by an angler in the Yellowstone Lake.

ⓐ a lake trout

ⓑ a grizzly bear

ⓒ a coyote

6. Lake trout are not easily found during the summer, when they live in waters _________ feet deep, far below the average depth most people fish.

ⓐ 10 to 20

ⓑ 30 to 50

ⓒ 50 to 100

7. A serious _________ in 1990s could have affected the dwindling population of cutthroat trout in Yellowstone Lake.

ⓐ introduction

ⓑ angling

ⓒ drought

8. The park service is trying to control the number of lake trout by focusing most of the _________ on lake trout.

ⓐ natural resource

ⓑ fishery budget

ⓒ park rangers

# Comprehension Questions

**Read the text again and answer the following questions.**

1. What has made it possible for the Yellowstone cutthroat to keep its genetic purity?

2. Why were the new regulations in 1975 effective in protecting the Yellowstone cutthroat population?

3. Why was the grizzly bear so dangerous to the Yellowstone's cutthroat?

4. What was the most probable cause for the presence of lake trout in Yellowstone Lake?

5. What consequences are expected to occur if lake trout are not controlled in Yellowstone Lake?

Student No. : ______________________ Name : ______________________

# Expanding Vocabulary

## 1 Each sentence contains an underlined word from the text, followed by three definitions. Put an √ next to the best meaning of the word as it is used in the sentence.

1. A lesser-known yet extremely significant accomplishment is the national park's role as a <u>sanctuary</u> for the genetically pure Yellowstone cutthroat trout.

___ ⓐ a nature reserve in which animals or plants are protected

___ ⓑ a building or room in which dead bodies are kept

___ ⓒ a charitable regard for the earth's endangered species

2. In the Western United States, where native fish have not <u>fared</u> well, the Yellowstone cutthroat is in better shape than most.

___ ⓐ expensed ___ ⓑ prospered

___ ⓒ charged

3. The fish is now a key part of the park's <u>ecological</u> balance.

___ ⓐ relating to the environment

___ ⓑ not wasting money

___ ⓒ contrary to the principles of logic

4. Unlike other cutthroat populations, the future of the Yellowstone subspecies appeared <u>assured</u>.

___ ⓐ feasible ___ ⓑ removable

___ ⓒ guaranteed

5. By the early 1980s, the restoration of Yellowstone Lake's cutthroat fishery was hailed as a major <u>conservation</u> success story.

___ ⓐ talk between people

___ ⓑ protection and preservation

___ ⓒ a doubt or objection

6. Lake trout are voracious predators of the cutthroat and were not supposed to be in Yellowstone Lake at all.

___ ⓐ craving food in large quantities

___ ⓑ eager or interested

___ ⓒ intensely angry

7. Lake trout prefer very cold water, so they appear in shallow water only just after the ice thaws in the spring and just before the lake freezes in the fall.

___ ⓐ breaks

___ ⓑ melts

___ ⓒ forms

8. The most plausible explanation for their presence is that an angler clandestinely planted them there once in a mistaken attempt to improve fishing.

___ ⓐ cleverly

___ ⓑ politely

___ ⓒ furtively

9. Since they can eat fish up to half of their body length, there aren't many cuts invulnerable to this.

___ ⓐ incapable of being damaged

___ ⓑ difficult to solve or deal with

___ ⓒ unable to get on together in harmony

10. The animal garnering the most concern is the park's grizzly bears.

___ ⓐ protecting

___ ⓑ collecting

___ ⓒ consuming

## 2 Choose the best word to fill in the blank.

1. Her performance was _________ as one of the best by most of critics.

ⓐ convinced ⓑ propagated
ⓒ acclaimed ⓓ diagnosed

2. Obese people are more _________ from diabetes and heart disease.

ⓐ in profusion ⓑ on probation
ⓒ in agreement ⓓ at risk

3. Environmentalists are calling for the new pesticide _________ to be strictly enforced.

ⓐ invention ⓑ regulations
ⓒ proclamation ⓓ provocation

4. The public want to protect their domestic industry from foreign _________.

ⓐ traders ⓑ predators
ⓒ executives ⓓ philanthropy

5. _________ of good diplomatic relations between South Korea and China would be a good thing for its own political sake.

ⓐ Destruction ⓑ Confrontation
ⓒ Restoration ⓓ Reservation

6. The resort is easily _________ by road, rail and air.

ⓐ accessible ⓑ invincible
ⓒ prompted ⓓ promulgated

7. The press had criticized her so often that in the end she had become _________ to bribery.

ⓐ congruent ⓑ immune
ⓒ consistent ⓓ confined

8. This special offer has been ________ designed for readers of Home magazine.

ⓐ intermittently ⓑ indifferently

ⓒ impromptu ⓓ exclusively

9. This has led scientists to ________ on the existence of other galaxies.

ⓐ depend ⓑ consummate

ⓒ ejaculate ⓓ speculate

10. The water was turned off for several hours each day during the ________.

ⓐ indignation ⓑ drought

ⓒ irrigation ⓓ jettison

# Listen & Write

**Listen to the recorded text and write a two- or three-sentence summary.**

## 1

In the Western United States, where native fish have not fared well, the Yellowstone cutthroat is in better shape than most. This comparative advantage exists largely because the heart of its range overlaps Yellowstone, where years of protection have isolated the fish from many problems faced by other native cutthroat subspecies.

---

## 2

By the early 1980s, the restoration of Yellowstone Lake's cutthroat fishery was hailed as a major conservation success story. But the cheering stopped in the summer of 1994, when rangers were presented with a lake trout by an angler who claimed it was taken from Yellowstone Lake. Park officials were dumbfounded. Lake trout are voracious predators of the cutthroat and were not supposed to be in Yellowstone Lake at all. A few days later a second lake trout was caught and reported. Fearing the worst, park officials set gill nets in the lake and immediately captured a few more.

---

## 3

The animal garnering the most concern is the park's grizzly bears. Yellowstone National Park's grizzlies have a limited menu of potential food sources compared with other bear populations. Wipe out the trout, and the survival of the entire Greater Yellowstone grizzly bear population may be in jeopardy. In a study done in the early 1990s, Dan Reinhart estimated 44 different bears were eating from spawning streams. This number may represent one-fifth of all grizzlies in the Greater Yellowstone ecosystem.

---

## Writing Assignment

Choose one of the following topics or titles as your unit writing assignment.

1. Nature and Men

2. Nature Conservation and People's Lives

3. Conservation or Development?

# Unit 10

## Diet Riot

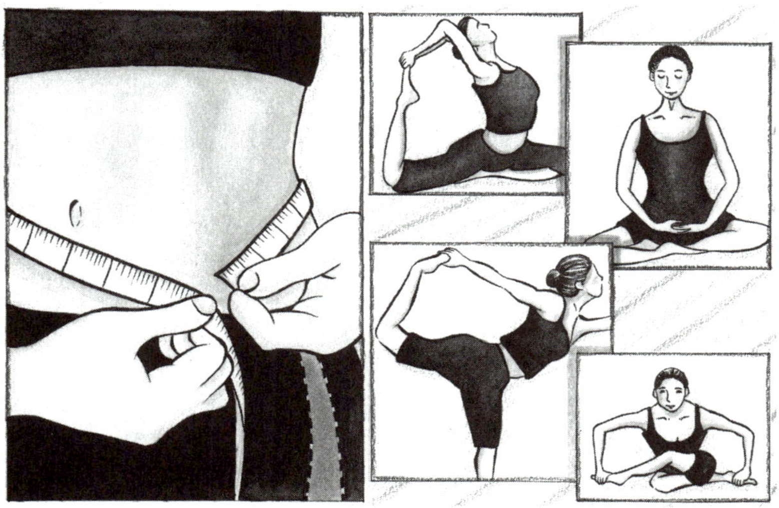

Look at the photos and think about the following questions.

1. Are you interested in losing weight? What have you been doing to lose weight? What do you think is the best way of losing weight?

2. Have you ever thought of the relationship between diet and health? Is diet good or bad for our health?

3. Collect as much information about effective diet programs or successful diet story from the newspaper or the Internet.

## Vocabulary Preview

**Here are some words and phrases from the reading. Put a check mark by the words you know. If you don' t know the meaning of a word, look it up in the dictionary.**

| | | |
|---|---|---|
| ___ 1. bulge | ___ 2. stroll | ___ 3. svelte |
| ___ 4. blurt | ___ 5. carbohydrate | ___ 6. addict |
| ___ 7. advocate | ___ 8. emphasis | ___ 9. trendy |
| ___ 10. pile | ___ 11. modify | ___ 12. aficionado |
| ___ 13. publicist | ___ 14. hospitalization | ___ 15. clinical |
| ___ 16. regimen | ___ 17. intake | ___ 18. hormonal |
| ___ 19. nutrient | ___ 20. impressive | ___ 21. counter |
| ___ 22. kidney | ___ 23. constipation | ___ 24. bristle |
| ___ 25. cholesterol | ___ 26. slap | ___ 27. guru |
| ___ 28. incorporate | ___ 29. avid | ___ 30. diagnose |
| ___ 31. remission | ___ 32. conceivable | ___ 33. diabetic |
| ___ 34. eliminate | ___ 35. refined | ___ 36. obese |
| ___ 37. adhere | ___ 38. obsess | |

## Skimming for Main Ideas

**Read the text one time quickly for the main ideas and put a check mark by the sentence that you think is mentioned in the reading text.**

___ a. More and more Americans these days have been interested in losing weight.

___ b. Most diet programs emphasize eating low-fat and high-protein food.

___ c. The effects of various diet programs have been evidenced by a lot of scientific research.

___ d. Weight Watchers, one of the diet programs, allows people to eat any food as long as they stay within their point total for the day.

# Read

## Diet Riot

*Everybody's trying to lose weight. but can getting that great body actually be bad for your health?*

In the battle of the bulge there's often no time for small talk. Suzanne Somers was strolling on the beach outside her Malibu home recently when Shirley MacLaine rushed up asking to know how the 53-year-old Somers kept herself svelte. "She said, 'Can you tell me about your program?'" recalls Somers with a laugh. "You know, not 'Hello,' but 'Can you tell me about your program?'"

Like MacLaine, Americans looking for a way to get or stay thin don't have to search far. These days, it seems, there are more diet books available than there are calories in a jelly doughnut. From *Atkins* to *The Zone*—to Somers's own Somersizing food-combining strategy described in her book *Eat Great, Lose Weight*—diet programs are popping up like oven-ready biscuits. And those who have found an effective way to downsize often are eager to spread the word. "I've lost weight on *the Sugar Busters*! diet," Elizabeth Taylor blurted out during an April *Good Morning America* interview. Matt LeBlanc credits a Friends friend for his eating habits. "Jennifer Aniston turned me on to the Zone," he told *PEOPLE* recently. Demi Moore, meanwhile, introduced Rosie O'Donnell to the *Carbohydrate Addict's Diet*, which the talk show host started last year. Said the 32-lbs.-lighter O'Donnell in April: "It's the first time I've kept weight off for that long a time."

With all the different plans around, there are plenty of conflicting theories. *Weight Watchers*, for example, advocates balanced meals based on a point system. Others, like Dr. Andrew Weil's *Eating Well for Optimum Health* and Dr. Dean

Ornish's *Eat More, Weigh Less,* put the emphasis on low-fat eating.

The most trendy at the moment are the *Zone*—which advocates a careful balance of carbohydrates, fat and proteins—and plans like Dr. Robert Atkins's *New Diet Revolution, Sugar Busters! and Carbohydrate Addict's,* which push a diet low in carbs but higher in protein. "You can tell people who are on the Atkins diet," says Weil. "They go right to the bacon. These are the same people who were on a low-fat diet and haven't been able to eat bacon for years, so they pile it on."

The latter plans are particularly popular in weight-obsessed Hollywood. "The majority of my clients right now want Zone-oriented kinds of meals," reports Mindy Lymperis, whose *Gourmet Grub to Go* delivers home-cooked meals to such stars as Kirstie Alley and Ali MacGraw. And in the past couple of years, says Kay Martin, whose *Kay's Gourmet Catering* in L.A. serves commercial shoots, "if you have a group of 50, you only need 25 bagels 'cause they don't eat them. Not anymore." Just ask 7th Heaven star Catherine Hicks, who recently lost 15 lbs. on a modified Zone diet. "I won't touch a piece of bread," says Hicks. "I've noticed I've become much thinner." "No bread," agrees composer and fellow Zone aficionado John Tesh. "I haven't had bread in two months. My energy is up and I've put on muscle."

But can dieting go too far? There were reports—denied by his publicist—that *Friends* star Matthew Perry's recent hospitalization was brought on by a high-protein diet. And critics question the lack of clinical testing behind many of these weight-loss regimens. According to the Atkins diet, the body will start burning fat if the carbohydrate intake is minimal; Barry Sears's *The Zone* refers to the favorable hormonal balance achieved by eating the right proportions of nutrients (30 percent protein, 30 percent fat, 40 percent carbohydrates). But despite the authors' scientific claims, "little research has been done on the various diets that are on the bestseller lists," says Bonnie Liebman, head of nutrition for the Center for Science in the Public Interest.

Which is not to say the results can't sometimes be impressive: Actress Connie

Stevens lost 20 lbs. in less than three weeks on the Zone, and NYPD Blue's Dennis Franz shed 35 lbs. last year on a modified Atkins plan. "Of course you can lose weight on diets that aren't good for you," counters Dr. Dean Ornish, whose low-fat, almost-vegetarian regimen has been followed by Laura Dem and Jane Seymour. "It's a great way to sell books to tell people what they want to hear, that steaks and ice cream are health foods. I'd love to tell people that they are, but they're not." In fact, experts caution that long-term use of high-protein diets—which are often high in fat—can lead to kidney damage and heart disease. (Bad breath, body odor and constipation are other possible side effects.)

Atkins fairly bristles when his diet is criticized as unhealthy. "There is no evidence of that whatsoever," he says. "I can find 20 studies that show an improvement in cholesterol levels with the Atkins diet and none that shows worsening."

Still, it isn't always easy sticking to such diets or keeping the weight off. Last October, Oprah Winfrey tried out the Carbohydrate Addict's Diet, which limits carb-rich foods such as bread and fruit to one "reward" meal a day. After a month she commented that she had lost 4 lbs.—and her patience. "Eventually you want some bread," she said on her show. "I was going to slap somebody for an apple."

So in April, Winfrey, who had previously tried Optifast, Weight Watchers, the Scarsdale Diet and Atkins, welcomed to her show food guru Dr. Weil. His moderate program of 50 to 60 percent carbohydrates (the less refined the better), 30 percent fat and 10 to 20 percent protein incorporates the traditional Mediterranean diet, which "happens to be my favorite way of eating," said Winfrey.

And it's a healthy way of eating, believes country singer Naomi Judd, who became an avid Weil devotee after being diagnosed with hepatitis C in 1990. "I eat a lot of fish," says the singer, whose illness is in remission. "He has taught me to incorporate soy into my diet. I eat very little red meat, maybe once every couple of months."

A health scare was also the wake-up call for onetime Designing Woman Delta Burke. Though she had dieted for years—"trying to be a size 6" through every conceivable program, she says—nothing worked until doctors told her in 1997 that she was diabetic. That led to a self-designed eating plan. "I have to have more protein because of the diabetes," she told *PEOPLE* last fall, "and I've just about eliminated white bread, rice and refined foods. I'm learning to pick and choose between my carbs." Now down to 150 lbs., 65 less than her peak weight of 215 lbs., she says happily, "I did it the right way, and it's stayed off."

Others have found their right way in programs such as *Weight Watchers* and *Slim-Fast*. "It's not about throwing out entire food groups," says former model Lauren Hutton, author of the new *Slim-Fast Body-Mind-Life Makeover*. "A can of Slim-Fast is healthier than the food that most people eat, which is fat-laden junk food." Indeed, a new study published in *Nutrition* magazine showed that a group of 134 obese Slim-Fast users kept an average of 10 lbs. off for more than five years.

A lifetime dieter, *Weight Watchers* spokeswoman Sarah Ferguson, the Duchess of York, has gone from 210 lbs. and a size 14 to her current size-10 frame. Because *Weight Watchers* allows any food as long as you stay within your point total for the day, Ferguson says it's not uncommon for people to approach her at restaurants and grill her about what's on her plate. "I say, 'I'm allowed to eat that, thank you very much!'" she says. "There's no such thing as a no-no food." Actress Fran Drescher, who joined *Weight Watchers* in 1993 and still adheres to its guidelines, agrees. "It's a lifestyle," she says. "It teaches you to be moderate."

Even so, in a world obsessed with both weight and trends, some foods will likely always go in and out of style. When word went around Hollywood a while back that drinking water at anything other than room temperature interfered with digestion, "you couldn't get cold water on a TV soundstage," caterer Mindy Lymperis recalls with a laugh. "They go through their fads."

## Reading for Detail

Test your understanding of this text by filling gap in each blank or answer - ing the multiple-choice reading comprehension questions without looking back at the text. Choose the best answer from the choices listed.

1. What is the title of a diet book written by Suzanne Somers?

   ⓐ Eat More, Weight Less

   ⓑ Eat Great, Lost Weight

   ⓒ Sugar Busters!

2. Rosie O'Donnell started the _________ Diet and lost 32 lbs.

   ⓐ Carbohydrate Addict's

   ⓑ Atkins's New

   ⓒ Slim-Fast

3. Which diet program emphasizes the careful balance of carbohydrates, fat and proteins?

   ⓐ the Zone

   ⓑ Weight Watchers

   ⓒ New Diet Revolution

4. What was the most probable reason of Matthew Perry's hospitalization?

   ⓐ a modified Zone diet

   ⓑ a high-protein diet

   ⓒ a low-carbs diet

5. Experts say that long-term use of _________ diets can cause kidney damage and heart disease.

   ⓐ high-protein

   ⓑ low-fat

   ⓒ low carbs

6. Which was Oprah Winfrey's favorite diet program?

ⓐ Weight Watchers

ⓑ Scarsdale Diet

ⓒ Dr. Weil's

7. After she tried to lose weight for years, Delta Burke suffered from ________.

ⓐ obesity

ⓑ diabetes

ⓒ high cholesterol

8. ________ makes it possible for people to eat any food as long as they stay within their point total for the day.

ⓐ Slim Fast

ⓑ Weight Watchers

ⓒ The Mediterranean diet

## Comprehension Questions

**Read the text again and answer the following questions.**

1. What are some of the most favorable diet programs by Americans these days?

2. What was the difference between Weight Watchers and Dr. Weil's program?

3. What was the scientific claim made by Barry Sears?

4. How did Dr. Atkins respond when his diet was criticized as unhealthy?

5. What was the effect of Slim Fast published in Nutrition magazine recently?

Student No. : ____________________ Name : ____________________

# Expanding Vocabulary

**1** Each sentence contains an underlined word from the text, followed by three definitions. Put an √ next to the best meaning of the word as it is used in the sentence.

1. In the battle of the <u>bulge</u> there's often no time for small talk.

___ ⓐ rudeness

___ ⓑ swelling

___ ⓒ extremely filthy

2. Weight Watchers, for example, <u>advocates</u> balanced meals based on a point system.

___ ⓐ recommends or supports

___ ⓑ moves or goes forward

___ ⓒ says with no preparation

3. Critics question the lack of <u>clinical</u> testing behind many of these weight-loss regimens.

___ ⓐ relating to office work

___ ⓑ genetically identical

___ ⓒ relating to medical studies

4. According to the Atkins diet, the body will start burning fat if the carbohydrate <u>intake</u> is minimal.

___ ⓐ a thing accepted

___ ⓑ inner part

___ ⓒ something on fire

5. Bad breath, body <u>odor</u> and constipation are other possible side effects.

___ ⓐ an arrangement

___ ⓑ a distinctive smell

___ ⓒ a bad condition

6. "I eat a lot of fish," says the singer, whose illness is in remission.

___ ⓐ official request

___ ⓑ lessening in force

___ ⓒ willingness to surrender

7. A health scare was also the wake-up call for onetime Designing Woman Delta Burke.

___ ⓐ mark or blemish

___ ⓑ short supply

___ ⓒ fright or panic

8. I've just about eliminated white bread, rice and refined foods.

___ ⓐ made bright

___ ⓑ excluded

___ ⓒ exclaimed

9. Actress Fran Drescher, who joined Weight Watchers in 1993 and still adheres to its guidelines, agrees.

___ ⓐ physically depends on

___ ⓑ objects to

___ ⓒ follows exactly

10. "Of course you can lose weight on diets that aren't good for you," counters Dr. Dean Ornish.

___ ⓐ opposes

___ ⓑ meets unexpectedly

___ ⓒ recites numbers

## 2 Choose the best word to fill in the blank.

1. Tony drove up in his ________ new sports car.

ⓐ downsized ⓑ svelte
ⓒ impressive ⓓ modified

2. She must be a shopping ________.

ⓐ devotee ⓑ scare
ⓒ advocate ⓓ addict

3. Boys are brainwashed into thinking that it's smart, ________, masculine to smoke.

ⓐ trendy ⓑ ashamed
ⓒ moderate ⓓ refined

4. He ________ out the rumor to his friends.

ⓐ strolled ⓑ spread
ⓒ blurted ⓓ commented

5. After his heart attack, the doctor put him on a strict ________.

ⓐ propaganda ⓑ digestion
ⓒ diabetic ⓓ regimen

6. Some foods will likely always go in and out of ________.

ⓐ country ⓑ remission
ⓒ style ⓓ trend

7. The new car design ________ all the latest safety features.

ⓐ stipulates ⓑ contaminates
ⓒ incorporates ⓓ strengthens

8. Her illness was _________ as a mild form of pneumonia.

ⓐ diagnosed ⓑ serious

ⓒ prompted ⓓ proved

9. She became _________ with the idea that she was being watched.

ⓐ involved ⓑ confessed

ⓒ obsessed ⓓ concerned

10. He tried every _________ combination of numbers.

ⓐ compatible ⓑ invincible

ⓒ conceivable ⓓ vulnerable

# Listen & Write

**Listen to the recorded text and write a two- or three-sentence summary.**

## 1

Like MacLaine, Americans looking for a way to get or stay thin don't have to search far. These days, it seems, there are more diet books available than there are calories in a jelly doughnut. From Atkins to the Zone—to Somers's own Somersizing food-combining strategy described in her book Eat Great, Lose Weight—diet programs are popping up like oven-ready biscuits. And those who have found an effective way to downsize often are eager to spread the word. "I've lost weight on the Sugar Busters! diet," Elizabeth Taylor blurted out during an April Good Morning America interview. Matt LeBlanc credits a Friends friend for his eating habits. "Jennifer Aniston turned me on to the Zone," he told PEOPLE recently. Demi Moore, meanwhile, introduced Rosie O'Donnell to the Carbohydrate Addict's Diet, which the talk show host started last year. Said the 32-lbs.-lighter O'Donnell in April: "It's the first time I've kept weight off for that long a time."

---

## 2

But can dieting go too far? There were reports—denied by his publicist—that Friends star Matthew Perry's recent hospitalization was brought on by a high-protein diet. And critics question the lack of clinical testing behind many of these weight-loss regimens. According to the Atkins diet, the body will start burning fat if the carbohydrate intake is minimal; Barry Sears's The Zone refers to the favorable hormonal balance achieved by eating the right proportions of nutrients (30 percent protein, 30 percent fat, 40 percent carbohydrates). But despite the authors' scientific claims, "little research has been done on the various diets that are on the bestseller lists," says Bonnie Liebman, head of nutrition for the Center for Science in the Public Interest.

---

## 3

A lifetime dieter, Weight Watchers spokeswoman Sarah Ferguson, the Duchess of York, has gone from 210 lbs. and a size 14 to her current size-10 frame. Because Weight Watchers allows any food as long as you stay within your point total for the day, Ferguson says it's not uncommon for people to approach her at restaurants and grill her about what's on her plate. "I say, 'I'm allowed to eat that, thank you very much!'" she says. "There's no such thing as a no-no food." Actress Fran Drescher, who joined Weight Watchers in 1993 and still adheres to its guidelines, agrees. "It's a lifestyle," she says. "It teaches you to be moderate."

---

# Writing Assignment

Choose one of the following topics as your unit writing assignment.

1. Is it good for health to lose weight?

2. My Favorite Diet Program

3. Korea Obsessed with Weight Loss

Unit 11

# The Conquest of Everest

Look at the photos and think about the following questions.

1. What do you know about Mt. Everest?

2. Do you know who conquered Mt. Everest for the first time? What do you know about them?

3. What are the benefits from climbing mountains?

## Vocabulary Preview

**Here are some words and phrases from the reading. Put a check mark by the words you know. If you don' t know the meaning of a word, look it up in the dictionary.**

___ 1. expedition
___ 2. blaze
___ 3. triumphant
___ 4. ridge
___ 5. boulder
___ 6. enigmatical
___ 7. ravage
___ 8. equipment
___ 9. assault
___ 10. impassable
___ 11. suppress
___ 12. stinging
___ 13. plaster
___ 14. binoculars
___ 15. vertical
___ 16. glisten
___ 17. ecstatically
___ 18. aglow
___ 19. tribute
___ 20. monarch
___ 21. clasp
___ 22. reflective
___ 23. inexorable
___ 24. symmetrical
___ 25. spectacular
___ 26. monotonous
___ 27. miscellaneous
___ 28. devout

## Skimming for Main Ideas

**Read the text one time quickly for the main ideas and put a check mark by the sentence that you think is mentioned in the reading text.**

___ a. The Everest expedition in 1953 was different from the previous ones in that it approached the peak from Tibet, not from Nepal.

___ b. On D-day the weather was not perfect. The sudden gales ravaged the base camp.

___ c. The expedition team at the base camp were excited by several encouraging factors such as good news from the South Summit.

___ d. The view from the Everest peak was not so spectacular, for it was too high for good landscape.

# Read

## The Conquest of Everest, 29 May 1953

**James (Jan) Morris**

*The successful 1953 Everest expedition was led by Sir John Hunt and approached the 29,002-feet-high peak from Nepal. Previous climbers had approached from Tibet.*

The masters of Everest, Hillary and Tensing, returned to this camp (22,000 ft) from the South Col yesterday afternoon in a blaze of sunshine and triumphant emotion, bringing their news with them.

It was a significantly beautiful day among the snows of the upper Western Cwm. All was crisp and sparkling, with the awful lock of Nuptse only faintly shining with the curious greasy sheen of the melting surface snow. From the ridge of Lhotse a spiral of snow powder was driven upwards by the wind like a genie from a bottle. From down the Cwm came from time to time a sudden thrilling high-pitched whistle as a boulder screamed down form the heights. Everest itself, its rock ridge graceless against a blue sky, was as hard and enigmatic as ever.

It was a day for great news. Here in the camp on the north side of the Cwm there was already yesterday morning a tension, nerve-racking and yet deliciously exciting. At 9 a.m. on the previous day, 29 May, the two summit climbers had been seen by their support group, Gregory, Lowe, and a Sherpa, already crossing the South Summit at about 28,500 feet, and going strongly up the final ridge.

The weather had been perfect, the gales of the preceding days which had so ravaged Camp VII on the South Col had died down. Hillary and Tensing were known to be two of the most powerful climbers in the world, and were using well-tested open-circuit oxygen equipment. Reports brought down from the South Summit by Bourdillon and Evans, who had reached it on 26 May in the expedition's first assault, seemed to show that the unknown final ridge was not impassable, though undoubtedly difficult.

Because of these encouraging factors, hopes at Camp IV were dangerously high, and the feeling of taut nerves and suppressed wild convictions were immeasurably strengthened when, just before lunch, five tiny figures were seen making their way across the traverse at the top of the face of Lhotse. They could only be the summit team and their supporters from the South Col. They were moving fast, and in three hours they would be in the Cwm. The camp was now alive with stinging expectation. Here in the camp Colonel Hunt sat on a wooden packing case, physically immobile, his waterproof hat jammed hard over his head, his face white with plastered glacier cream. Four or five of the climbers vacantly fingered newspapers in the big pyramid tent. One man sat outside with binoculars reporting the progress of the descending party.

'They must be getting to Camp VI,' the watchers said. 'They are hidden behind that serac [ice-pinnacle] with the vertical crack in it—you know the one.' 'Two of them are sitting down now they are up again.' 'Only another hour to wait. What are the odds?' At last, soon after 1 : 30, just as the radio was announcing the reported failure of the assault, the party emerged above a rise in the ground 300 yards or so above the camp, their blue windproof jackets sharp and cheerful against the glistening snow. Hillary and Tensing were leading. All at once the excitement that Everest had been climbed spread through the camp.

There was a sudden rush up the snow slope in the sunshine to meet the assault party. Hillary, looking extraordinarily fresh, raised his ice axe in greeting. Tensing slipped sideways in the snow and smiled, and in a trice they were surrounded. Hands were wrung ecstatically, photographs taken, there was the whirr of the ciné camera, and laughter interrupted congratulations.

Hillary and Tensing, by now old climbing colleagues, posed with arms interlocked, Hillary's face aglow but controlled, Tensing's split with a brilliant smile of pleasure. As the group moved down the hill into the camp a band of Sherpas came diffidently forward to pay tribute to the greatest climber of them all. Like a modest monarch, Tensing received their greeting. Some bent their bodies forward, their hands clasped as in prayer. Some shook hands lightly and delicately, the fingers scarcely touching. One veteran, his pigtail flowing, bowed to touch Tensing's hand with his forehead.

'We so far forgot ourselves,' wrote an English climber of an earlier generation, 'as to shake hands on the summit.' This expedition so far forgot itself that everywhere on fancied that sunglasses were steaming embarrassingly: and suddenly, as if spontaneously, each climber, Hillary and Tensing the first of them, turned to Colonel Hunt, reflective in the background, and shook his hand in recognition of the truth that in a team venture of great happiness and success his has been the friendly hand which inexorable as it seems had led the expedition to success.

In the pyramid tent, over an omelette served on an aluminum plate, Hillary told the story of the final climb···It was at 11 : 30 a.m., 29 May 1953, that they stepped at last on to the snow-covered final eminence of Everest.

Hillary describes this as 'a symmetrical, beautiful snow-cone summit'—very different from the harsh rock ridge which is all that can be seen from below, The view was not spectacular. They were too high for good landscape, and all below looked flat and monotonous.

To the north the route to the summit on which pre-war Everest expeditions pinned their hopes looked in its upper reaches prohibitively steep. Tensing spent the fifteen minutes on the summit eating mint cake and taking photographs, for which purpose Hillary removed his oxygen mask without ill effect. Tensing produced a string of miscellaneous flag and held them high, while Hillary photographed them. They include the Union Jack, the Nepal flag, and that of the United Nations. Tensing, who is a devout Buddhist, also laid on the ground in offering some sweets, bars of chocolate, and packets of biscuits.

# Reading for Detail

**Test your understanding of this text by filling gap in each blank or answer - ing the multiple-choice reading comprehension questions without looking back at the text. Choose the best answer from the choices listed.**

1. Who were the first human beings to mount the top of Everest? Choose two.

___ ⓐ Hillary
___ ⓑ Lowe
___ ⓒ Tensing

2. Who spotted the two summit climbers on May 28?

___ ⓐ their support group
___ ⓑ reporters
___ ⓒ Colonel Hunt

3. What kind of equipment did Hillary and Tensing use for climbing?

___ ⓐ oxygen equipment
___ ⓑ screw driver
___ ⓒ flippers

4. What did Hillary do when he met the assault party?

___ ⓐ He slipped sideways in the snow and smiled.
___ ⓑ He raised his ice axe in greeting.
___ ⓒ He vacantly fingered newspapers.

5. Who led the Everest expedition in 1953?

___ ⓐ Gregory
___ ⓑ Hillary
___ ⓒ Hunt

6. Why did the Sherpas move diffidently forward when Hillary and Tensing move down the hill into the camp?

___ ⓐ to pay respect to them

___ ⓑ to take a phonograph

___ ⓒ to pass over foods

7. How long did Tenzing and Hillary stay on the summit?

___ ⓐ 10 minutes

___ ⓑ 15 minutes

___ ⓒ 20 minutes

8. How was the route to the summit on the north?

___ ⓐ rather smooth

___ ⓑ with melting snow

___ ⓒ very steep

# Comprehension Questions

**Read the text again and answer the following questions.**

1. How was the weather on May 29, 1953?

2. What was the message of the reporters who reached the South Summit?

3. Exact when did Hillary and Tensing get to the top of Everest?

4. Which flags were held high on the summit of Everest?

5. What did Hillary and Tensing do on the summit?

Student No. : ______________________ Name : ______________________

# Expanding Vocabulary

**1** Each sentence contains an underlined word from the text, followed by three definitions. Put an √ next to the best meaning of the word as it is used in the sentence.

1. The successful 1953 Everest <u>expedition</u> was led by Sir John Hunt and approached the 29,002-feet-high peak from Nepal

___ ⓐ an investigation of a crime scene

___ ⓑ knowledge in a particular job

___ ⓒ an organized journey for a particular purpose

2. Everest itself, its rock ridge graceless against a blue sky, was as hard and <u>enigmatic</u> as ever.

___ ⓐ very charming and appealing

___ ⓑ mysterious and difficult to understand

___ ⓒ very serious and earnest

3. The weather had been perfect, the gales of the preceding days which had so <u>ravaged</u> Camp VII on the South Col had died down.

___ ⓐ devastated

___ ⓑ went wild

___ ⓒ whitened

4. The camp was now alive with <u>stinging</u> expectation.

___ ⓐ sharply painful

___ ⓑ criticizing

___ ⓒ parsimonious

5. There was a sudden rush up the snow slope in the sunshine to meet the <u>assault</u> party.

___ ⓐ harassment ___ ⓑ offence

___ ⓒ attack

6. They were too high for good landscape, and all below looked flat and monotonous.

___ ⓐ very boring

___ ⓑ completely controlled

___ ⓒ full of excitement

7. To the north the route to the summit on which pre-war Everest expeditions pinned their hopes looked in its upper reaches prohibitively steep.

___ ⓐ very expensive

___ ⓑ very strong and determined

___ ⓒ rising at a sharp angle

## 2 Choose the best word to fill in the blank.

1. He returned home as a _________ general.

ⓐ triumphant ⓑ gregarious
ⓒ graceless ⓓ brilliant

2. The hospital has set up a special fund to buy new _________.

ⓐ pinnacles ⓑ photocopiers
ⓒ binoculars ⓓ equipment

3. The line of the Lincoln High football team was _________, but our hard-running backs managed to find a way through it.

ⓐ impossible ⓑ incremental
ⓒ impassable ⓓ prohibitive

4. The police have been accused of _________ evidence relating to the trial.

ⓐ depressing ⓑ oppressed
ⓒ suppressing ⓓ compressing

5. Nothing in nature is truly _________ even the mountains are in constant movement and change.

ⓐ brutal ⓑ immortal
ⓒ incidental ⓓ immobile

6. By the time the lifeboat arrived, the ship was almost _________ in the water.

ⓐ frozen ⓑ vertical
ⓒ dismantled ⓓ windproof

7. The _________ has the theoretical power to dismiss the government.

ⓐ monarch ⓑ summit
ⓒ general ⓓ boulder

8. She _________ the baby to her bosom.

ⓐ accosted ⓑ clasped
ⓒ glittered ⓓ clipped

9. After listening to the pleas for clemency, the judge was _________ and gave the convicted man the maximum punishment allowed by law.

ⓐ enigmatic ⓑ thrilling
ⓒ delicate ⓓ inexorable

10. The lawyer said the suspect was a(n) _________ Muslim who had lived in the United States for five years and was faint with hunger from fasting during Ramadan.

ⓐ devout ⓑ tranquil
ⓒ spontaneous ⓓ eminent

# Listen & Write

**Listen to the recorded text and write a two- or three-sentence summary.**

## 1

It was a significantly beautiful day among the snows of the upper Western Cwm. All was crisp and sparkling, with the awful lock of Nuptse only faintly shining with the curious greasy sheen of the melting surface snow. From the ridge of Lhotse a spiral of snow powder was driven upwards by the wind like a genie from a bottle. From down the Cwm came from time to time a sudden thrilling high-pitched whistle as a boulder screamed down form the heights. Everest itself, its rock ridge graceless against a blue sky, was as hard and enigmatic as ever.

## 2

Because of these encouraging factors, hopes at Camp IV were dangerously high, and the feeling of taut nerves and suppressed wild convictions was immeasurably strengthened when, just before lunch, five tiny figures were seen making their way across the traverse at the top of the face of Lhotse. They could only be the summit team and their supporters from the South Col. They were moving fast, and in three hours they would be in the Cwm. The camp was now alive with stinging expectation. Here in the camp Colonel Hunt sat on a wooden packing case, physically immobile, his waterproof hat jammed hard over his head, his face white with plastered glacier cream. Four or five of the climbers vacantly fingered newspapers in the big pyramid tent. One man sat outside with binoculars reporting the progress of the descending party.

## 3

Hillary and Tensing, by now old climbing colleagues, posed with arms interlocked, Hillary's face aglow but controlled, Tensing's split with a brilliant smile of pleasure. As the group move down the hill into the camp a band of Sherpas came diffidently forward to pay tribute to the greatest climber of them all. Like a modest monarch, Tensing received their greeting. Some bent their bodies forward, their hands clasped as in prayer. Some shook hands lightly and delicately, the fingers scarcely touching. One veteran, his pigtail flowing, bowed to touch Tensing's hand with his forehead.

# Writing Assignment

Choose one of the following topics as your unit writing assignment.

1. Joyful Experiences of Mountain Climbing

2. Why do people try to conquer nature?

3. Famous Climbers I Know

# Unit 12 Food FAQs

Look at the photos and think about the following questions.

1. How do you choose your foods? On what basis? Nutrition or taste?

2. Cite some traditional Korean foods which you think are good for health. Have you tried them? How about the taste?

3. What is your favorite exotic dish? Where is it from? Do you think other people like it, too?

## Vocabulary Preview

**Here are some words and phrases from the reading. Put a check mark by the words you know. If you don' t know the meaning of a word, look it up in the dictionary.**

| | | |
|---|---|---|
| ___ 1. convert | ___ 2. nutritional | ___ 3. increment |
| ___ 4. potassium | ___ 5. proportion | ___ 6. obesity |
| ___ 7. hybrid | ___ 8. clinician | ___ 9. legume |
| ___ 10. Mediterranean | ___ 11. deist | ___ 12. quintessential |
| ___ 13. ingredient | ___ 14. artery | ___ 15. expectancy |
| ___ 16. candidate | ___ 17. mortality | ___ 18. coronary |
| ___ 19. ecosystem | ___ 20. anthropologist | ___ 21. cardiovascular |
| ___ 22. genetic | ___ 23. indigenous | ___ 24. lipid |
| ___ 25. metabolism | ___ 26. propensity | ___ 27. trajectory |
| ___ 28. chronic | ___ 29. lethal | ___ 30. insecurity |
| ___ 31. ironically | ___ 32. junk | ___ 33. wholesome |

## Skimming for Main Ideas

**Read the text one time quickly for the main ideas and put a check mark by the sentence that you think is mentioned in the reading text.**

___ a. The US Dietary Guidelines have very practical values to Americans, satisfying all nutrition professionals.

___ b. The life expectancy of the Mediterranean people has decreased and many of them are suffering from obesity, but the Mediterranean diet is still popular among those who try to eat right.

___ c. Arctic people eat a great deal of meat, but they have a low blood lipid level. It is because of their vigorous physical activity under their frozen environment.

___ d. The lack of proper nutrients occurs only in poor countries, where more than 3.7 million children died in 2002.

# Read

## Food FAQs

*Eating a healthy diet is hard work. There are hundred of guides out there—often providing conflicting instructions. Deciding what advice to take means wrestling with a number of tough questions.*

### Q: How is science converted to dietary advice?

To make the jump from scientific data to specific recommendations for a healthy diet—that everyone should now eat nine servings of fruit and vegetables a day, for instance—that scientists on the US Dietary Guidelines Advisory Committee turned to computer modeling.

They mixed and matched foods from the traditional groups—fruits, vegetables, grains, meat and beans, dairy foods, fats and sweets—to come up with combinations that met nutritional requirements put forward by the Institute of Medicines' Dietary Reference Intakes. This gave them a series of food patterns for a range of daily calorie intake levels from 1,000 to 3,200, in increments of 200. These model diets were designed to boost nutrients that are often too low in US diets, such as vitamin E, calcium, magnesium, potassium, fibre and vitamin A.

In a twist, the nutritional value of each food group was calculated to reflect what Americans actually eat, rather than as a simple average of all the foods in the group. For example, broccoli accounts for more than half of the greens Americans eat, and spinach about a fifth, according to the 1999~2002 Natural Health and Nutrition Examination Survey. So the value of the greens group as a whole was calculated as having 0.53 of the nutritional values of broccoli and 0.20 of the combined average of other greens.

Committee members say that this approach allowed them to make recommendations with practical value to Americans, who are not likely to radically shift the proportions of foods they eat within the food groups.

But the result did not entirely satisfy nutrition professionals. Dena Bravata, a physician and obesity researcher at Stanford University in California, says that although the guidelines are valuable she would have preferred them to be "based more on the scientific evidence rather than this hybrid approach." The average US diet is hardly ideal, she says, and knowing what food combinations are optimal would allow patients and clinicians to create individualized diets based on the best available evidence.

The approach has its disadvantages, the committee admits. Many people in the United States don't get enough vitamin E, for example, so one might have expected the guidelines to recommend eating more nuts and oils, which are rich in this vitamin. But Americans eat very few real nuts (peanuts, although popular, are actually legumes) and use oils that are low in vitamin E, so nuts and oils ended up with low vitamin E scores in the computation. This meant acrobatic accounting to boost other food groups with average levels of vitamin E.

### Q: Which countries or cultures have the best diets?

Several groups are in the running. Many people consider the traditional Mediterranean diet to be one of the healthiest. But times are changing. With the globalization of the food market, processed foods are creeping into traditional diets at the same time that physical activity is declining in many parts of the world. More and more, the people with the best diets are those who make a concerted effort.

In collaboration with the Harvard School of Public Health, Oldways, a Boston-based non-profit organization that promotes healthy eating, has assembled several traditional deists into food guided pyramids, following the shape of the official eating guide set out by the US Department of Agriculture. These take traditional dietary patterns into account, as well as data from clinical and epidemiological research.

The Oldways Mediterranean pyramid is based on the diet of Greece, Italy, Portugal and Spain around 1960, a time when people in those countries lived longer than their northern European neighbors and were less likely to develop heart disease. Their daily fare included whole grain bread, pasta, rice, fruit, beans vegetables, cheese, yoghurt and that quintessential Mediterranean ingredient, olive oil. They also ate fish, poultry, eggs and sweets weekly. But red meat, with this artery-clogging saturated fat, was consumed less often.

Today, these eating habits are gradually being abandoned, and at the same time the Mediterranean advantage in life expectancy has decreased and obesity is on the rise. But the diet itself remains popular among those who try to eat right. As a result, diet-conscious people in places that lack strong nutritional traditions may be candidates for the best eaters today. "Middle-aged, educated women in California eat particularly healthy diets," says Martijn Katan, nutrition scientist at the Wageningen Center for Food Sciences in the Netherlands.

If effort is essential, certainly few countries have tried harder to eat right than Finland. In the early 1970s, Finnish men had the highest rate of heart disease in the world. Their diet consisted of large amounts of whole milk, cheese and salt, with very little in the way of fruit and vegetables. A national programme of education and changes to the food supply over three decades has vastly improved the national diet. Today, the mortality from coronary heart disease in working-age men has been reduced to a quarter of what it was in the 1970s.

**Q: There must be a natural diet for humans — what did we evolve to eat?**

The good news is that evolution teaches us that humans can eat just about any mix of the basic food groups. During evolution, we have colonized almost every ecosystem on Earth, and adapted to what was available; from Arctic populations eating almost exclusively animal protein, to villagers in the peaks of the Andes living largely on grains and cereals.

We evolved as "flexible eater," say William Leonard, an anthropologist at Northwestern University in Evanston, Illinois, and an expert on diet in evolution. Taken from this evolutionary vantage point, arguments in diet books over whether a low-fat, high-carbohydrate diet is better than high-protein low-carb diet make no sense, he says. Alice Linchtenstein, a cardiovascular researcher at Tufts University School of Medicine in Boston who sat on the scientific committee that produced the 2000 US dietary guidelines, agrees. "A variety of diets are possible from an evolutionary point of view," she ways.

The bad news is that evolution has also left us with a genetic legacy: our brains and genes are hardwired to seek out as much energy as possible for the least physical effort. This served humans well during millennia when starvation was a constant threat to our survival but is not adapted to the modern world where high-calorie foods are a phone order or shot drive away.

Evidence for this can be found in the Arctic, for instance. Indigenous people who maintain a traditional lifestyle eat a great deal of meat, yet they have a low blood lipid level, which is a risk factor in heart disease, and enjoy good cardiovascular health. The explanation, Leonard proposes, is that their rate of metabolism is raised as a result of vigorous physical activity and in response to their frozen environment. But their relatives who have adopted a more sedentary way of life, and a Western diet that has more processed foods and less meat, have significantly increased blood lipid levels and higher rates of obesity and cardiovascular disease.

Such findings have implications for the hunt for 'fat genes'. Although some genes may be linked to the risk of getting fat, obesity is less the result of individual genetic propensities than of the shift in environmental conditions, says Ricardo Uauy, an expert on public health and nutrition at the London School of Hygiene and Tropical Medicine. "The past 50 years is too short to modify our evolutionary trajectory."

**Q: Do we have enough of the right kind of food for everyone on the plant?**

Certainly if one considers the world's chronically undernourished, who now number some 850 million people, the answer is no. But the surprise is that many of those who are better off or who live in countries with abundant food supplies still fail to get the nutrients they need, and may even be overweight in spite of this.

The problem of chronic hunger occurs almost entirely in poor countries. The condition is particularly lethal to children, of whom more than 3.7 million died in 2002 from the health consequences of being underweight. Another estimated 850,000 died because their diet—although sufficiently rich in calories—did not contain enough vital components such as iron, vitamin A and zinc.

The lack of proper nutrients is also a phenomenon in wealthy countries, where food insecurity, if not starvation, is surprisingly common. In the united States for example, 12.6 million households (about 11%) fall short of basic food needs at some point during the year. In about a quarter of those cases, people fail to get government food aid or find private charities to make up the difference, and so go hungry.

Ironically, poverty and obesity often go hand in hand in developed countries. "Obesity is a disease of the poor in rich countries, whereas in poor countries obesity is a disease of the rich," says Katan.

A key factor is that junk food tends to offer the most calories for the least money. "This is the single most important factor influencing food choice," says Marion Nestle, professor of nutrition, food studies and public health at New York University. In US supermarkets, for instance, a 270-calorie doughnut cost about 75cents, the same as 125-calorie apple.

The ready availability of processed and fast foods in many corners of the globe is now making them the natural choice, particularly for the poor and uneducated. Apart form being cheap, they have a natural appeal, Nestle says. "Eating highly refined food rich in sugar and fat is a kind of joy, which poor people do not frequently have," she says.

Although it is true that wholesome foods are also available throughout the industrialized world, evidence suggests that even slight inconvenience is enough to put people off buying them. A representative study involving participants in the US food-stamp programme shows that people tend to buy more fruit the closer they live to a supermarket.

## Reading for Detail

**Test your understanding of this text by filling gap in each blank or answer-ing the multiple-choice reading comprehension questions without looking back at the text. Choose the best answer from the choices listed.**

1. What kind of vegetables do Americans eat most?

ⓐ broccoli
ⓑ spinach
ⓒ lettuce

2. What kind of food is recommended to get enough vitamin E?

ⓐ whole grain bread
ⓑ nuts
ⓒ cheese

3. According to the passage, Finnish diet in the early 1970s consisted of ______

ⓐ fruit
ⓑ vegetables
ⓒ cheese

4. What made the Finnish diet improve greatly in the 1990s?

ⓐ intake of large amounts of dietary food, fruit, and vegetables

ⓑ a national education programme and changes to the food supply

ⓒ government aid of finding private charities to supply the food

5. Arctic people eating exclusively animal protein have a low blood lipid level as a result of ____

ⓐ vigorous physical activity

ⓑ adopting a more sedentary way of life

ⓒ genetic transmission

6. Why did 3.7 million children die in 2002?

ⓐ Their diet did not contain enough iron, vitamin A and zinc.

ⓑ They got health problems resulting from being underweight.

ⓒ They did not respond properly to their frozen environment.

7. How many people didn't get enough nutrients?

ⓐ 50 million

ⓑ 850 million

ⓒ 3.7 million

8. According to the passage, the problem of chronic hunger occurs in

ⓐ poor countries

ⓑ wealthy countries

ⓒ both

## Comprehension Questions

**Read the text again and answer the following questions.**

1. Why did the scientists mix foods from the traditional group?

2. What kinds of food were included in the traditional Mediterranean diet?

3. What does the term "flexible eater" mean?

4. Why do diets in wealthy countries show a lack of proper nutrients?

5. What are the main reasons people buy junk food?

Student No. : ______________________ Name : ______________________

# Expanding Vocabulary

**1** Each sentence contains an underlined word from the text, followed by three definitions. Put an √ next to the best meaning of the word as it is used in the sentence.

1. This gave them a series of food patterns for a range of daily calorie intake levels from 1,000 to 3,200, in increments of 200.

___ ⓐ average heights

___ ⓑ amount of money

___ ⓒ increases in value

2. Committee members say that this approach allowed them to make recommendations with practical value to Americans, who are not likely to radically shift the proportions of foods they eat within the food groups.

___ ⓐ extremely

___ ⓑ excitedly

___ ⓒ wirelessly

3. Although the guidelines are valuable, she would have preferred them to be "based more on the scientific evidence rather than this hybrid approach.

___ ⓐ chemical

___ ⓑ involving water

___ ⓒ mixture of things

4. This meant acrobatic accounting to boost other food groups with average levels of vitamin E.

___ ⓐ reduce

___ ⓑ amplify

___ ⓒ eradicate

5. More and more, the people with the best diets are those who make a concerted effort.

___ ⓐ working together

___ ⓑ concrete

___ ⓒ conclusive

6. A Boston-based non-profit organization that promotes healthy eating has assembled several traditional deists into food guided pyramids,

___ ⓐ congregated

___ ⓑ attacked

___ ⓒ combined

7. Today, the mortality from coronary heart disease in working-age men has been reduced to a quarter of what it was in the 1970s.

___ ⓐ justice

___ ⓑ corruption

___ ⓒ death

8. The bad news is that evolution has also left us with a genetic legacy: our brains and genes are hardwired to seek out as much energy as possible for the least physical effort.

___ ⓐ legitimacy

___ ⓑ folk tale

___ ⓒ inheritance

9. The lack of proper nutrients is also a phenomenon in wealthy countries, where food insecurity, if not starvation, is surprisingly common.

___ ⓐ investigation

___ ⓑ vulnerability

___ ⓒ confidence

## 2 Choose the best word to fill in the blank.

1. Many reasons for that center around its excellent ________ profile; primarily, it's low in calories, low in fat, especially saturated fat.

ⓐ clinical ⓑ healthy
ⓒ diabetic ⓓ nutritional

2. A really fat woman cries on stage talking about how she has been mistreated by people because of her ________.

ⓐ propensity ⓑ obesity
ⓒ potassium ⓓ undernourishment

3. The book was a ________ of four authors.

ⓐ hybrid ⓑ collaboration
ⓒ conversion ⓓ proportion

4. He'd concocted the most amazing dish from all sorts of unlikely ________.

ⓐ ingredients ⓑ fibers
ⓒ flavors ⓓ proteins

5. The third ________ is a dark horse. She's new to politics and is just beginning her campaign.

ⓐ charity ⓑ component
ⓒ candidate ⓓ grain

6. The world's tropical forestlands are among nature's richest and most biologically diverse ________.

ⓐ anthropology ⓑ evolutions
ⓒ wastelands ⓓ ecosystems

7. Each person's _________ code is unique except in the case of identical twins.

ⓐ lipid ⓑ lethal

ⓒ genetic ⓓ chronic

8. Dr. Heymsfield knew that some people do have _________ that use calories at a low rate.

ⓐ expectancy ⓑ colonies

ⓒ clinicians ⓓ metabolisms

9. A lot of Korean people these days are suffering from financial _________.

ⓐ increments ⓑ insecurity

ⓒ mortality ⓓ saturation

10. It's _________ that she became a teacher, because she used to hate school when she was a girl.

ⓐ ironic ⓑ sedentary

ⓒ implicational ⓓ indigenous

# Listen & Write

**Listen to the recorded text and write a two- or three-sentence summary.**

## 1

They mixed and matched foods from the traditional groups—fruits, vegetables, grains, meat and beans, dairy foods, fats and sweets—to come up with combinations that met nutritional requirements put forward by the Institute of Medicines' Dietary Reference Intakes. This gave them a series of food patterns for a range of daily calorie intake levels from 1,000 to 3,200, in increments of 200. These model diets were designed to boost nutrients that are often too low in US diets, such as vitamin E, calcium, magnesium, potassium, fibre and vitamin A.

## 2

Evidence for this can be found in the Arctic, for instance. Indigenous people who maintain a traditional lifestyle eat a great deal of meat, yet they have a low blood lipid level, which is a risk factor in heart disease, and enjoy good cardiovascular health. The explanation, Leonard proposes, is that their rate of metabolism is raised as a result of vigorous physical activity and in response to their frozen environment. But their relatives who have adopted a more sedentary way of life, and a Western diet that has more processed foods and less meat, have significantly increased blood lipid levels and higher rates of obesity and cardiovascular disease.

## 3

The lack of proper nutrients is also a phenomenon in wealthy countries, where food insecurity, if not starvation, is surprisingly common. In the united States for example, 12.6 million households (about 11%) fall short of basic food needs at some point during the year. In about a quarter of those cases, peoplefail to get government food aid or find private charities to make up the difference, and so go hungry.

# Writing Assignment

Choose one of the following topics as your unit writing assignment.

1. My Favorite Food

2. My Own Healthy Diet

3. What is a natural diet for humans?